You Were Born A Warrior

A Near Death Experience

By

Ryan J. Rampton

Dedication

**For my children,
grandchildren,
and
family;
you mean everything to me.**

Better than a thousand hollow words, is one word that brings peace.

---Buddha

Take sips of this pure wine being poured. Don't mind that you've been given a dirty cup.
---Rumi

You are a warrior. You have had many battles already. May you find one part of this book that uplifts you and brings you peace.

---Ryan Rampton

Ryan Rampton
2403 W 1700 S
Syracuse Utah 84075
801-309-6219
www.youwerebornawarrior.com

Ordering Information:
Quantity sales. Special discounts are available on quantity purchases by corporations, associations, and others. For details, contact the publisher at the address above.
Orders by U.S. trade bookstores and wholesalers. Please contact: Tel: (801) 728-0421; or visit www.ryanrampton.com.

Printed in the United States of America

You Were Born A Warrior
Introduction

My name is Ryan Rampton. I died in 2001 by electrocution. I went to heaven and met God. I had to make a choice if I was going home with Him or if wanted to come back to earth. I chose wrong and for my punishment, I had to write this book.

Just kidding. I came back to learn, serve, and make a difference.

I am not your typical spiritual person. I joke too much, sin too much, and am somewhat irreverent. With all my faults, I do love God with all that I am. I will testify of the love that we are and the perfect love God is, perfect and unconditional beyond our understanding. I am going to tell you about my visit with God, what He showed me, and what I learned there and after through some very sacred spiritual experiences.

You may say I had some opposition in writing this book and you would be correct. Honestly, if I had known just how hard it would be, and how much opposition I would go through, I may have called it quits. I'm glad I didn't know, but a warrior for God knows there are hard things to do, and does them anyway. Plus, I was commanded by an angel to write this, so no matter what, I wasn't going to quit.

It has taken me five years to get this written. I have learned so much about myself the last five years while I have been writing. I swear the opposition threw everything they had against me to keep me from writing: from attacks on my character, lies and false rumors, losing my job, losing relationships, health problems, suicidal feelings and attempts, to horrific accidents.

I feel like I fought a battle and barely survived. But this is God's book, not mine. I'm writing to testify of His love and compassion for us. I am here to tell you that you are enough and perfect, and to let God into your heart to fill that void in your soul. Nothing will fill it no matter how hard you try, until you fill it with God. Remember your own being is divine. You are part of God. It's not about learning; it's about remembering

I am a miracle. I should not be alive. It is only through God's power I am here. What I am about to show you will demonstrate that God's miracles did not stop in the Bible with Daniel in the lion's den or with Shadrach, Meshach and Abednego in the fiery furnace.

Chapter 1
Indestructible

April 22, 2019

I had just finished speaking about my Near Death Experience in Las Vegas Nevada at a conference and had a book signing for the first edition of this book. I had no idea I would be adding to it today.

I was driving home to Syracuse, Utah from Las Vegas on I-15 traveling north. I had an incredible download for my next book and I was dictating it into my phone in a voice memo.

It was such a powerful download and I knew it would be a powerful book about God. I finished the thirty-minute recording and thought I better say a prayer of thanks.

I pray often and it is usually with my eyes open and taking to Father like I would talk to someone I love. I thanked Father for my life, my blessings, my ability to serve, and the download I had just received. I also asked for protection. Because I knew how much opposition I had in writing this over the last five years, I knew the opposition would try and stop me from writing my second book.

I had just finished my prayer and I was enjoying the scenery. It was a beautiful spring day. The sun was shining, the red rock hills looked so amazing with the emerging green of spring and the beautiful blue sky and white puffy clouds.

I was feeling so blessed. My iPhone was on a magnetic mount on my dash. I reached forward and closed the app I had been using to record my book.

I looked up to the road and saw the most unbelievable image. My brain could not even process what I was seeing. Horror flooded my mind as I watched a truck drop from the sky in front of my car. It landed upside down and skidded toward me in my lane. I was traveling north doing about 80 mph in the fast lane. I didn't even have much time to react, maybe a fraction of a second as I stomped on the brakes.

The red truck exploded around me as my SUV came apart. The impact was horrific. I remember the airbag being deployed and I wondered why I didn't feel it and why it didn't hit my face. It was like it came up against a wall as it deployed around me. My vehicle continued to move forward and I had the thought to steer it to the right shoulder of the road to avoid being rear ended. I came to a stop next to a concrete barrier. I was alive.

I didn't understand how, but I was alive. I looked around my car and was amazed at the damage. There was hardly anything left. The roof was gone, the seat next to me was impaled and crushed by metal. The dash was crushed around me trapping me in the vehicle.

I felt for any injuries and didn't feel any. I could tell I was in shock but I appeared to be uninjured. A man from another car had stopped and ran up to check if I was hurt. I told him I was okay. He asked if I could get out, but I told him I was trapped in the car; the door was jammed and the dash held my legs.

The man returned a few minutes later with a water bottle and handed it to me through my broken windshield. I was inspired by the kindness from complete strangers. It testifies how connected we all are. We are one. When you help someone else, you are helping yourself; when you hurt someone else, you are hurting yourself; when you forgive someone else, you are forgiving yourself.

The gentleman brought back another guy and they were able to pry my door open and help pull me out of the wreckage.

I was amazed at the damage around me. I couldn't believe how I had survived. I was in shock. I had no pain. I didn't have a seat belt mark from the sudden stop or an airbag burn from it exploding and hitting me in the face. My knees didn't even hurt from the dash crushing around them, I felt shaken and had a headache, but other than that I felt okay.

A semi-truck driver who had also hit the red pickup truck told me what he saw. He said the red pickup was traveling south on I-15, had crossed the media, hit the concrete barricade and shot up in the air about twenty feet before coming down and landing upside down in my lane. Seconds later my vehicle hit it and it exploded and rolled over my vehicle. He was sure that both the drivers of the red pickup truck and the white SUV, which was me, were both dead. Miraculously, we were both okay and walking around.

I was a full-time firefighter and saw many terrible accidents. Looking at the damage done to my vehicle and the kinetic force that destroyed my vehicle and even bent my cell phone and shattered the screen, I couldn't understand how my body came out with only a few cuts from broken glass. The brain and the heart are both suspended in your body and not held into place with muscles or tendons like many other organs. They are easily damaged in sudden stop accidents. The brain can suffer damage much like a ball being thrown at a wall; it will bounce off one side of the skull and rebound into opposite side and injure both sides of the brain. The heart is suspended in your chest by two large blood vessels which can easily be torn when the heart is slammed into the ribs after a sudden stop, often resulting in death.

I couldn't understand how I escaped those injuries let alone why my legs were not hurt from the dash crushing around them. It was like I was encased in a force field. I couldn't think of any other explanation. It was a bonified miracle.

Here is the most important part of the accident; I was saved by the power of God and His angels. Everyone I have told the story to has tried to use their mind to rationalize what happened and try and explain how I am still alive and uninjured. It is a miracle just like Daniel and the lion's den or Shadrach, Meshach and Abednego in the fiery furnace. We believe in the Bible when we hear of these miracles but we often explain away the miracles that happen around us. I am truly blessed and I recognize God's hand in keeping me safe and unharmed. His power is matchless.

You, like me, have been through hard things and come out the other side still willing to go on, still willing to fight this battle called life. You, like me, "Were Born A Warrior." Thank you fellow warrior for the light for reading my book and helping me share my message. I love you and honor the part in you where God dwells.

I have included some of the photos from the accident so you can see with your own eyes and hear with my words the power of God.

I testify to you that I am a miracle because I have been saved many, many times, and that I have a mission and a work to do. I am a messenger from God proclaiming His love for you. I have been saved and protected so I may do His work and tell of His love. I am here to remind you how much you are loved, and that there is a divine eternal soul living within you.

Accident Photos

Accident Photos

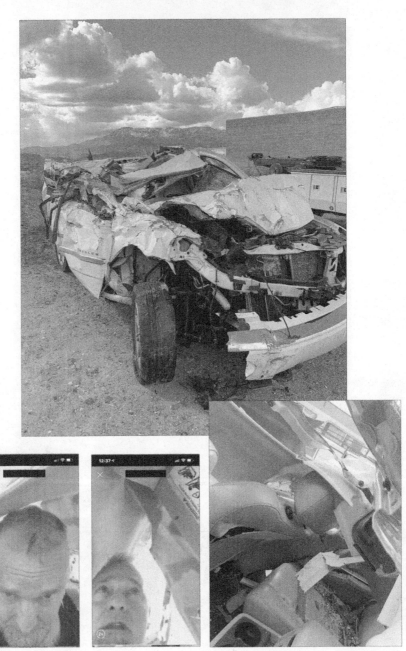

Chapter 2
Finding Faith in Tragedy

October 19, 2018

Twenty-five years ago today, I was a firefighter for Layton City. We responded to a mobile home fire. It was a horrible tragedy where three small children were trapped in a trailer that was fully engulfed in flames. We were able to knock down the fire and get the three children out but they were unconscious and unresponsive because of smoke inhalation.

The paramedics were able to resuscitate the eighteen-month-old, while the five-year-old sacrificed her life by laying on top of the other two kids trying to protect them, the four-year-old was resuscitated en route to the hospital on the life flight helicopter. Christina, the four-year-old was put into a medically induced coma for seven months and when she awoke was 98% brain dead. She lived eight more years then passed.

The other night my girlfriend and I went to dinner at Applebee's. A waitress started talking to us and somehow it came up that I had been a firefighter. She asked whom I had worked for and I said, Syracuse, Layton, and Murray Fire Departments. She asked when I had worked at Layton, I said, 1993 to 1998. She said, "Oh I bet you were on my fire." I said, "You had a fire?" She said yes, my mobile home off of 193." I instantly choked up, my voice became thick with emotion and I said, "Not the one the kids died in?"

Her eyes filled with tears, and she said, "Yes those were my babies." I started to cry uncontrollably. I couldn't believe how much emotion came up about that fire. I had buried it, pushed it down deep inside. I was a new rookie firefighter and had never seen children die before, let alone to pull out three bodies from a fire.

I remember suffering from PTSD and not understanding why I was feeling the way I was. One time my daughter got hurt when she was a baby. She cried for only two minutes and I cried and shook for two hours. My wife thought I had lost my mind.

My new friend Angie was the mom of these children and also our server at Applebee's. She invited me to go to the grave of her two girls that had died and witness her putting flowers on the graves. I have never met a stronger woman or someone that is so grateful for the one son she was able to keep. She has a positive loving outlook on life. Often times we focus on what we have lost and not what we still have, and what we are blessed with.

How often do we focus on the negative and all the terrible things that have happened instead of the blessings we still have? For the last twenty-five years, I carried this loss in my heart as a firefighter and the emotions that came up the last couple of days have almost been crippling. I cannot imagine losing two children. I got to talk to the son we saved on FaceTime and he was so grateful to Layton fire department for saving his life which he expressed to me. I am proud to represent Layton Fire Department and the amazing Firefighters that I worked with that help make a difference in this family's life.

I have focused and thought about this for the last 25 years but I always remembered the two we lost not the one we saved. Their family helped me realize how amazing God is and the blessings we can focus on instead of the losses. The boy now has three children of his own and Angie has beautiful grandchildren because we were able to save her boy.

Chapter 3
Writing

I started writing this book in the spring of 2013. I had about two chapters written and felt like I was doing pretty well. I was at work at my desk and the laptop I was writing my book on, was sitting on a table behind me. I was diligently working on my work computer doing some Photoshop work on some images when I heard a crash. I turned around and saw my laptop had crashed into the wall about five feet away from the table where it was sitting on.

I couldn't understand how it got there from that far away; even if it fell off the table it would have fallen right by the table, not across the room. I felt a chill in the air and the hairs on my neck stood up. I didn't feel safe, I looked around the room and no one was there. I thought; calm down, there is no one here. I walked across the room and picked up my laptop. The screen was broken and it wouldn't turn on. I didn't want to lose what I had written so I called my buddy who fixed computers and asked him if he could pull the chapters off from my book, that was the only thing I cared about.

My friend's name is Jason and is such a good man. He has one of the best hearts I had ever known. He was just that type of selfless guy that would do anything for you. He agreed to take a look at my computer. I told him I was writing a book and wanted to recover what I had written. I dropped the computer off to him and he called me the next morning. I said, "Hey buddy! Done already?" He said no I need to talk to you. I asked, "What's up?" He said, "What in the hell are you writing?" I said, "It's about my Near Death Experience, Why?" He emphatically said, "Write your damn book!"

I was kind of shocked to hear my friend swear, I asked, "Why do you say that?" He said that he had a dark spirit show up at his house in the middle of the night and woke him up and told him that if he helped me write my book the spirit would attack his family. So he repeated, "Write your damn book if I am going to put my family at risk you better finish this book. He said he jumped out of bed and put his arm to the square and commanded the spirit in the name of Jesus Christ to depart and it left, but he told me my book was important.

I won't tell you how many times I was attacked or all of the opposition I had in writing this book because I want to focus on the light not on how to fight the darkness. That will be in another book to come.

I will, however, share some stories about how many times I was protected and saved from death before I actually died and how God was saving me to be able to complete my mission, plus other stories of miracles while serving God.

Chapter 4
Letting the smoke out

The pain was unbearable. The electricity violently buzzed every cell of my body filling every cell with agonizing pain. I was literally frying. Black smoke was billowing out of my mouth. "Oh my God, I'm going to die" I screamed in my head. My heart was frozen along with the rest of my muscles. I couldn't even move my eyes to see if help was near.

That was when I died and met God. No kidding I went to heaven, much to the surprise of anyone who knew me. The funny thing was that God was not what I expected. He was pure love and joy. There was no judgment because I was a sinner or a disappointment because I was not righteous enough. He was as excited to see me as I was Him.

I thought my sins were beyond redemption. No, I've never murdered anyone, even though I thought about it a few times, maybe even planned it out in my head, but could never actually go through with that. I was a big enough sinner already, I did not need to add murder to the long list of the horrible things I've done. As it was, I assumed I was going to burn in hell for all eternity.

But that is not what happened. God stood with me and showed me my life through His eyes. He showed me how much he cared. He carried me in time of trouble; he protected me in times of sin. I did not feel worthy of this love, this adoration. I secretly hated myself, I was such a disappointment. I had expected so much out of myself, and I let me down.

I felt my sins were cancer eating at my soul. I tried everything to get rid of the cancer of self-hatred; denial, indifference, outright rebellion, repentance, religion, therapy, surrender, indulgence to excess trying to burn it out, but nothing helped. I just continued to self-destruct and hate myself.

But you would never know it, on the outside I was the life of the party. Everyone wanted to be me, except me....

I went from self-loathing to perfect acceptance and love for myself just being near God. I knew God loved me! It was amazing! It was healing! How could this be? No seriously, this flew in the face of everything I had been taught about God. My mind was blown. I felt like nothing that happened in my mortal life could have any affect or effect on me. I was completely healed.

I never wanted to leave God's presence. I was home and back to where I belonged. No more pain, no more sorrow only love. It was like a drink of the sweetest, coldest spring water after a lifetime in the desert.

After I came back to earth, I struggled until God gave me purpose. I was told by an angel to paint a portrait of my soul. Only part of that portrait is my near death experience but it was definitely a point of focus. So here is the unvarnished raw version of my life and experiences with and without God.

Chapter 5
The Journey

I want to tell you about my journey in learning about my eternal soul and the warrior within. I was born into a religious house with parents who believed in God and attended church regularly. I was taught right from wrong, and I believed in God and loved him. I saw many of dark spirits and was tormented by them on a regular basis until I was about 16 years old. I was always scared at night and would often have visits by two ghosts that lived in our house. My four-year-old self-named them "Very Good" and "Of Course". You couldn't say those words without me freaking out and telling you not to say their names! My parents thought this was cute, I thought it was serious and I couldn't understand why they laughed at me.

As I grew up, I was very spiritual and tried my best to be good and worthy of God's blessings. I was always taught that I had His love, and He loved everyone, but His blessings were only saved for His favorites, the righteous. I wanted so badly to be righteous. I craved being one of God's favorites. I knew I was special and I was meant for great things, but every time I failed, I lost a little more of my self-worth. I became a little less confident in knowing that I was good, and I felt tainted from a very young age. I knew there was something wrong with me, but if I could just try a little harder and be a little better, I would be loved and accepted.

I would have terrible dreams at three years old where I would wake up screaming and shaking. I would dream that a huge tire the size of a house was crushing me. I would babble that I wouldn't make it home, it was too hard, and I was so scared. My parents had no idea why I had these dreams and what was wrong with me, so I spent many nights coming into their room scared out of my mind. I knew from an early age my earthly mission was difficult and that the opposition was like a huge black tire that was trying to crush me.

All of our experiences are for our good and our learning. What I am about to tell you had nothing to do with me being a victim, it all was perfect for me to learn and grow. I love my Mom and I am so grateful for everything she did for me.

When I was four years old I had an experience with my Mom that would change my perception of myself for the next fifty years and possibly my entire life. It was deep-seated and went sub-conscious. Between birth and five years, we form our basic personality, our fears, our self-worth, and our strengths. People often require years of therapy to overcome childhood trauma, but we all have some.

I was a little boy of four who had been put to bed about seven in the evening. I woke up about eight and had to go to the bathroom. The bathroom was right next to my bedroom so I threw off the blankets and crawled out of bed. My little bare feet went shushing across the linoleum floor, I couldn't have carpet because I was allergic to everything. I was constantly on oxygen and medications for my asthma and allergies, and a lot of my early life I had to live in an oxygen tent or was constantly going to the doctor or the hospital.

I padded my way to the bathroom door and slowly turned the brass knob. I cracked the door and looked in through the crack, someone was in there. It was my Mom, and she was just getting out of the shower. She had pulled the curtain back and the steam billowed out of the shower surrounding her in mist. I stared transfixed. I had never seen my Mom naked. I was allowed to be in the tub with Dad but never my Mom. I remember seeing her and freezing in place as I peeked through the crack. I wasn't even sure what I was looking at except it was different than how Dad or I looked.

She noticed the door open and saw me peeking in. Her face went bright red and suddenly she was mad at me. She screamed, "Did you get your eyes full you little pervert? She grabbed a towel and wrapped herself up, and I let go of the door handle and started running toward my room. I forgot all about having to go pee. I was in bad trouble for something because I had never seen Mom this mad before. She stormed out of the bathroom wrapped tightly in her white towel, came into my room and slapped me across the face. I burst into tears and she screamed at me again. "You little pervert did you like what you saw? You are a naughty boy.

I was so scared and I buried my head in my pillow as my Mom continued to yell at me and call me names I didn't understand. I only knew she was really mad. I felt shame for the first time in my life, and it had something to do with seeing her naked. I felt shamed and that I was bad and would never be good. There was something wrong with me. I never even got out of bed again to go pee. I woke the next morning soaked to the core and smelling of urine. I knew I would be in trouble again and I agonized on telling my Mom. I was scared to even see her. I knew I was bad and she was just going to even be madder at me for peeing the bed.

A few years later I was the victim of sexual abuse. I was abused for a few years before it stopped, but this also made me feel like somehow it was my fault. I was wrong and bad and somehow caused the other person to do that to me.

I grew up feeling like I was wrong on a deep level. I remember getting baptized when I was eight years old and going into the bishop for my worthiness interview. I told the bishop I didn't think I should be baptized because I was a pervert. He asked me if I knew what that word meant, and I told him I'm not sure but I think it has something to do with seeing someone naked. He smiled at me with the kindest eyes I had ever seen. He was a very nice man with a slight speech impediment. He always had a little bit of a lisp that sounded like he had a little too much spit in his mouth.

He and his brother owned a very successful furniture store named RC Willey. Warren Buffet later bought the business and this amazing bishop went on to rise to higher callings in the church. He told me I was good and not a pervert, and asked me why I thought I was one. I told him my Mom called me that. I didn't dare tell him that I was being molested. He would tell me I was bad if

I told him that. He smiled kindly and said, "I'm sure your Mom didn't really think that about you. I think you are a good boy and you love the Lord." That man gave me courage and made me feel like maybe I wasn't so bad even with all the things that had happened to me. But as I got older and made more mistakes, it solidified my belief that I was bad and a pervert and I deserved the things that happened to me.

Years later I had an experience with the Lord where He showed me what had happened to my Mom when she was a little girl which explained her reaction to anything sexual. My heart broke for my Mom and I understood why she would lash out that way. I had compassion and love for her on a deeper level, and I wanted to go back in time and protect her and keep her from having the terrible experience that caused her to treat her precious little boy that way.

I understand that it was part of what I chose to learn here on earth, part of the cross I bear, part of the lessons that teach me what I am not. I learned shame over and over throughout my life, and I learned the opposite of what I am. My spirit is glorious, it is light and goodness, but I had to learn shame and a feeling I would never be enough to really appreciate what I was.

Chapter 6
What we are not

Part of what we came to learn was what we are not. You don't know what health is until you are sick. You don't know what love is until it is taken away and you feel your heart breaking. The contrast teaches us what we are. I was a very sick little boy, and my brother used to joke about me being "bubble boy". There was a movie about a boy who lived his life inside a bubble because he had no immune system and everything would make him sick. I was not nearly that sick, but I spent most of my time in an oxygen tent because my asthma was so bad. I also had a poor immune system and would catch everything except a baseball. I was sick and weak.

My parents thought I would not grow to adulthood but die from all of the problems I was born with. I remember fighting for every breath and always felt like I was drowning, that I could never get enough air. I was always exhausted fighting for life, for each breath of air.

I had to learn the opposite of what my spirit was, I believe that is why we are here. To learn about ourselves and the challenges and talents we chose for our major battles. The talents we were given help us overcome, uplift others and make the world a better place. The challenges help define us, shape us, and give us greater appreciation and gratitude for what we are and what we have been blessed with. We wanted to know the opposition. We wanted to be tried, tested, and put in the hot water of life to see just what kind of tea is in our bag.

I believe some of us chose lessons that are exactly the opposite of what our spirit is. For example, if you are a judgmental person who often criticizes others for their faults, maybe your highest self, your spirit, is one of the most compassionate spirits there is. Maybe you wanted to know "what you are not" just so you can really know and appreciate what you are.

My poor mother sacrificed her sleep, her health, and most of her sanity to care for me. She would stay up all night thumping on my back to break up the mucous and would give me nebulizer treatments so I could keep breathing. It was a battle for both of us. The pediatrician often told my mother to prepare for my passing, that I would not make it. Everyone was sure I would die, all except my Grandpa Rampton. He would give me a blessing and proclaim that I had to make it because I had such an important mission for the Lord.

I was weak, sick, scared and pitiful. I grew up despising my sickness, and weakness. I wanted to be strong, manly, and powerful not a weak wimpy sensitive kid. I longed to be the hero, the knight in shining armor, the kind of man that other men looked up to. I was none of that. I was pitiful and that was perfect. Perfect for my growth and my appreciation of what I was before earth and what I would become more like in my later years.

Now that I have a muscular body and have competed in bodybuilding competitions I try and create a balance between the weak, and sensitive little kid that still lives in me and the tough muscular exterior. I constantly tell my ego to go stand in a corner as I try and be humble, and prayerful. It is a juggling act to move forward with confidence and determination to win, and stay humble, and thankful for what the Lord has blessed you with. The trick is to stay grateful and recognize where our blessings come from.

Even though my Mom reacted poorly when I surprised, embarrassed, and whatever emotions went through her head when I saw her in the bathroom, she was the most dedicated loving Mom I could have asked for. The funny thing is my mom doesn't even remember the incident. It wasn't a defining moment for her like it was for me.

My Mom was inspired to take me to a man who did acupressure or foot zones. He cured me of my asthma within a few years, and I started to get better. I was still super scrawny and sick, though I never got picked for sports or asked to do athletic things, I was still a pretty happy child. We traveled a lot with my Dad being an airline pilot and spent a lot of time up at the lake in my Dad's boat.

Chapter 7
The Skunk and the Broncos

I used to love and ride my dirt bike. I had a Yamaha YZ125 and I rode it all around my Dad's rental property, which was about three acres. There were many hills and jumps that I would bravely "catch a little air" when I flew up and over them, I loved that feeling, I felt free and powerful. I was so surprised my worried mother was ever talked into letting me buy the bike in the first place, but if she could see me acting "dangerously" she would have a heart attack. I remember my Dad taking my side and telling her I would be all right. I loved the confidence he showed in me. I felt proud and manly.

I was twelve years old and at this point, I was really trying to be "righteous". I was attending church and was trying my best to repent and keep the commandments. I felt very spiritual like I had a purpose and a special mission. I had received a blessing of protection after I had been possessed and taken over by an evil spirit when I was eleven. I was praying and reading my scriptures daily. I struggled daily to find my worth and feel worthy and good enough for God.

I struggled in deciding if I was going to include what I had written about being possessed at eleven and all of the attacks by evil spirits, but I decided to focus on the light and the good. I will have another book that deals with what happened to me and how I was attacked and how to clear and defeat all kinds of negative spirits and energies. I have done so much clearing of negative spirits my step-grandchildren call me grandpa ghost hunter.

One day I was jumping one of the dirt piles, on my dirt bike, and being a little daredevil when I crashed and dumped the bike. I was trying to catch my breath after it was stolen from me by the impact of my chest with the handlebars and landing on my back with a hard thump into the ground when I heard a cry like a baby in pain. I lay there on the hard ground with my ears straining to hear again what I thought I just heard. My ears pricked up and I listened; There it was again, a sad and mournful cry.

I scrambled on my hands and knees to the top of the dirt pile and found a juvenile skunk that had its leg caught in a muskrat trap. It must have hurt the skunk something fierce as it was wailing in pain, and my tender heart broke because I felt so bad for it. I dropped down on my knees praying to God to help me save this poor little creature. I prayed that I would be able to walk up to the skunk and release it from the trap without being attacked by the wild little animal. I prayed that the skunk would be calm and not be afraid of me so I could save its life, I knew all you needed was faith. I had faith, and I knew I was special. I didn't listen for an answer. I didn't know how, but I felt confident that God would protect me on this special mission of charity and love.

I rose from my knees and walked slowly toward the skunk one tentative step at a time, speaking soothing words, "Don't worry little guy, God sent me to save you." I said with a smile, "I am here to rescue you." I believed with all my heart that I would be able to save the hurt little thing.

I took a step, and then another, dirt clods breaking under my feet. I was so close I could see how frightened the skunk was. He was looking at me with black trusting eyes but still unsure of my intentions. I kept speaking soothingly to it, "It's okay. God sent me to help you." I said with soft reverence, "Don't worry you will be free in a second." I remembered reading about Daniel in the lion's den and how God protected him and I was sure he would do the same for me with this harmless little creature. After all, it wasn't a lion.

I was about two feet from it, my heart bursting with love when the skunk turned its back on me, and I thought, "That's kinda rude." Then it raised its tail and blasted me in the face with this oily liquid that burned like gasoline. I screamed and fell backward scrambling like an upside-down crab to get away from the little demon. "It burns so bad!" I thought. Then the smell hit me. I had smelled plenty of skunks in my days growing up in farm country, but *never* up this close. It was overwhelming! It was worse than when my older brother made me eat his gym socks. The burning on my face was nothing compared to the smell! I wanted to vomit and rip my nose off at the same time!

I jumped up and ran in circles trying to run from the smell, screaming at the top of my lungs when I thought of my Mom. "She will help me! She will know what to do!" I ran for my tipped over dirt bike, picked it up, mounted it, and after about three kicks it roared to life.

I sped home driving on the road illegally instead of going through the fields. If a cop wanted to stop me and give me a ticket I would just hug him and contaminate him for life!

I spied my house quickly approaching. I sped onto the front lawn hardly allowing the bike to stop before I leaped off it, vaulted the front steps, threw open the front door, and made my grand entrance into the kitchen.

"Mom! I wailed, I got sprayed by a skunk!!!" But before I said the words, her nose already knew. She pulled an awful face scrunching her nose and face into a contorted position and yelled, "God Lord, Ryan, you stink to high heaven! Get out of my house and go hose yourself off out back!" She grabbed her broom and began to sweep my bottom out of her kitchen and out the back door.

"A skunk sprayed me!" I protested in my best-wounded little boy's voice, not the manly teenager that was just jumping a dirt bike.

"I can smell that. Good Lord, Ryan, you better not have permanently stunk up the house, or you will be sleeping outside for the next three months!" She hollered as she slammed the back door leaving me to the garden hose and the cold springtime water that would be coming out of it.

A window opened up on the back of the house and her voice sailed out, "I'll throw you out a bottle of dish soap

and a brush. We are going to have to bury your clothes. Strip down to your skivvies and make it snappy."
I was still crying as I held the garden hose in one hand and started to undress with the other. I was wearing my favorite silk Denver Broncos jacket that I had gotten for Christmas the previous December. "Mom, can't you wash my clothes and get the skunk out of them? I don't want to bury my jacket." I pleaded.

"You should have thought of that before you got yourself sprayed by a skunk. That jacket and those clothes will have to go in a hole in the ground. That smell will never come out." She yelled as dish soap and a brush came flying through the window and landed at my feet.

I reluctantly removed my clothes and piled them up as I stood in my "tighty whities" shivering as I eyed the garden hose like a poisonous serpent. It being early spring I knew this was going to be very cold. I finally turned on the hose and directed the stream of insult to add to my injury onto my body. It was so cold it took my breath away.

"Use that soap and that brush." The voice tumbled out of the window again as I laid down the hose and grabbed the bottle of Palmolive and the brush and began to suds myself all over. "Don't forget your hair! That is where most of the smell will set up shop! We may have to shave you bald!"

"Oh no!" I thought with terror. "Not my hair!" There is nothing worse than telling a pre-teen or a teenager of the eighties that you are going to cut their hair. Goodbye coolness and hello dorksville! I couldn't allow that to happen. I began to scrub with renewed vigor scrubbing from head to foot until my skin was a bright pink.

One time, about three years earlier, I was forced to stay with my Uncle Dennis when my parents and my older brother went to Sweden. My little sister and I were judged to be "too young" to be allowed to go. My Uncle Dennis was a religious tyrant with ideas of hellfire and brimstone oozing from his pores like a lumberjack sweats. He took one look at my "David Cassidy" hair after my parents dropped me off, and said, "You need a haircut, I don't know if you are a girl or if I should buy you a dog tag, but either way, it's gone." I was drug off, protesting and pleading, to the barbershop where they gave me a nice 1950's buzz cut. I think I wore a hat for a year after that waiting for my hair to grow out. I'm surprised that I even got possessed that next spring, evil spirits obviously don't have any fashion sense. You think they would pick a body with cool hair if given a choice.

I walked to the house dripping wet calling, "Mom I think I'm clean." My Mom threw open the door sniffed me and scrunched her face in disgust. "Good Lord Ryan, you better pray tomato juice takes the smell out or I'm getting the hair clippers." And she marched me off to the bathroom.

 "At least I will get a warm bath after the cold garden hose," I thought. I started to draw a bath when she announced. Hold on and just stand in the tub. I've got three quarts of tomato juice we will pour over you first. I shut off the water and stood in the tub.

"Strip off those wet underwear and put them in this garbage bag," she insisted.

"Mom," I protested, "I'm not getting naked when you are in here.

She rolled her eyes, handed me a garbage bag and set three quarts of tomato juice on the counter. I waited for her to close the door and pulled off the wet "butthuggers" as my brother called them, usually just before he gave me a wedgie. I opened the first jar of juice and poured it over my head. The cold acidic juice made my mouth water and my body shiver. I thought, "What a waste of good tomato juice."

"Make sure you scrub with a brush!" Mom's voice intruded through the closed door.

"I grabbed the brush and tried to scrub but my skin was so raw and tender that I resorted to a washcloth and rubbed myself using the softer cloth with the remaining jars of juice. When I was finally done and had rinsed off with warm water, I started the bath. It felt so good to sink into the warm water after going through the cold hose and cold juice. I rewashed everything with soap and shampoo and got out and dried off. I wrapped the towel around me and called my mother. "

"Mom, I think I'm clean and don't stink anymore," I said.

She opened the door sniffed me a couple of times and announced, "Nope you still have a lingering skunk smell. Get back in the tub."

"But Mom," I protested, "I don't want to. I'm clean enough." I firmly stated.

"OK, Ryan, I guess we can just shave off your skunk hair then." She said and opened up the drawer that held the clippers.

"Wait!," I protested, "I can do better," and started to fill the tub again. She shrugged, turned, went out, and closed the door.

I opened the cupboards and found the "Comet" cleanser. "This will work!" I thought. I remembered using it as a kid to wash my face hoping it would somehow age me, make me look older, and not be the baby-face my older brother called me. I sprinkled it all over my body washed with the washcloth again and then used shampoo and soap one more time.

"I'm not going to bathe for a month after this," I vowed.

This time I passed inspection with flying colors. I guess the comet wouldn't make me look more mature, but it did bleach the skunk out of me. The hardest part was digging the hole and burying my favorite clothes. I've often wondered ever since then when my Dad would complain the Broncos are playing like a "bunch of skunks," that was somehow my fault.

I remember feeling forsaken by God, and in church that Sunday when we were learning about Jesus in the Garden of Gethsemane, Jesus said, "Father, Why hast thou forsaken me?" I wanted to shout out to the teacher, "Yeah, he forsook me too! He let a skunk spray me right in the face!" But I was a little too embarrassed to relate that story. I remember developing a grudge against God at that point. I had prayed! I had faith! I believed! I didn't understand how it works serving God. I hadn't waited for an answer from God that it was okay to approach the skunk, I just prayed and assumed He would protect me.

My older and hopefully wiser self wants to say, "Ryan, God has never forsaken you. Sometimes He just lets you learn hard lessons, or sometimes, He just let's nature take its course. He wanted to teach you it's not righteousness or your idea of wickedness that protects you, blesses you, forsakes or curses you. It's your independence that allows nature to take its course. If God had whispered to you to save that skunk, you would have been protected. You decided to do that on your own. It was your independence that got you sprayed. It was your independence that you think is wicked also. When you think you are being righteous you feel superior, when you think you are being wicked you feel inferior or have self-hatred. Your independent nature is what swings you from self-righteousness to self-hatred, not God nor His opinion, His love for you never wavers, and it is always deep love. He is quite fond of you."

Chapter 8
Blessing

I got a blessing when I was twelve from a man in our church. He was called a patriarch and he gave patriarchal blessings. The recorded blessing tells you of your spiritual lineage and of gifts and talents you have and acts as a guide for you to follow in your life. It told me many marvelous things and told of my future activities and how much the Lord loved me and how much protection I had over me. I read that blessing over and over growing up. There was one part in there that always puzzled me at that age. It said that I was assigned to go on a mission. It then went on to say if that time comes that it is possible for me to do so in this probation (life) I would be a great missionary and teacher because I perfected these talents before I ever came to this earth.

I couldn't understand why I wouldn't be able to go on a mission at nineteen. All Mormon boys were expected to go on a mission. It was unthinkable for God telling me that it wouldn't be possible in this life, so I figured maybe there would be a war and I would be fighting in it. I had no idea I would get my girlfriend pregnant at eighteen and we would get married. I feel like the Patriarch was connected to God and God told me what I needed to know. I always thought it was amazing how well God knew me to know what I would choose. I didn't understand at that time how God is outside of time, and knows Alpha to Omega, the beginning and the end. He knew me at five and at fifty, He knows everything I will ever do, and He loves me anyway. He loves my faults and my strengths.

I grew up learning to love God and tried my best to be good. I was drawn toward sex from an early age. I would touch myself often and think about sex, after all, I was a "pervert". I started to have sex around age sixteen. I was programmed to do things to bring me shame and make me feel bad and unworthy, this is part of what I came here to learn. I didn't know that I just thought there was something wrong with me and I was bad. I didn't think I would make it home to God. I would live an eternity in hell because I couldn't control my urges and desires, I had no self-mastery and I was bad.

Because I tried and failed to be good, I slowly started becoming less active in the church. Church made me feel dirty and wrong, even more than I already did so I began to avoid it and put other things in my life.

I married my girlfriend and we had a baby six months after our wedding. Sean my oldest son, came into my life. I was a dad at nineteen, trying to raise a family. I got accepted to the Air Force Academy, and I wanted to be a fighter pilot and fly jets. My Dad was an airline pilot and I wanted to be like him. I found out the vision requirements, being 20/20 or better, kept me out of the pilot's seat. I could be a navigator, but not a pilot like I wanted. I decided to take my full ride scholarship to Weber State University and work on my pilots' license and become a commercial pilot as my brother did. I ended up only going to school two semesters because I had to work full time to provide for our new family. I could have had all my dreams regardless of my obstacles, but at the time I didn't have the skills to overcome them. I just gave up.

It seemed like all my dreams were dying as I realized how bad I had messed up and ruined my life. I would never be a pilot or get my degree. I had to drop out of college and work a low paying job doing construction to be able to pay for the hospital bills and buy food. I began to realize what I loser I was. My parents were ashamed of what I had done. I wasn't going to be a pilot. Everyone was disappointed with me, especially me.

I found myself in a marriage to a girl I hardly knew, and I began to resent her for my predicament. Instead of seeing how blessed I was and making the best of my situation I blamed her and began to look to other women to make me feel loved. I had affairs on her, one after another. I treated her poorly and made her feel like she wasn't a good wife. She felt unhappy and had affairs on me in retaliation for my affairs. When one of us was trying, the other wasn't, we lived a vicious cycle of hurting the other partner.

After fifteen years of marriage, we finally decided we wanted to be sealed as a family in the Mormon temple. This is a goal of almost all Mormons. To go to God's highest kingdom you must be married for time and all eternity in the temple. So that's what we worked so hard to achieve. I thought this would fix everything, fix my broken unworthy self-image, and fix my wife. It would solve everything, and it did for a couple of months.

I had a bishop who I had repented to for having affairs on my wife. I worked really hard to be forgiven and repent for the wrong I had done to be worthy to go to the temple with my wife and be sealed as a family. After I had gone through the repentance process and had been reinstated to full membership, the bishop called me on the phone. I was so excited to finally be worthy to get married in the temple. Instead of telling me I had been accepted and could get married in the temple, he informed me that he was going to recommend that I be ex-communicated from the church.

I was shocked and asked, "What for?" He told me that he had gotten my records back from church headquarters and read that I had repented to my former Bishop Sanders that I had fondled a fifteen-year-old girl. He called me a child molester and said the church didn't allow child molesters in the church. I couldn't even talk for a minute I was so shocked.

I finally managed to say, "Bishop D., do you know how old I was when I repented to Bishop S. about that? I was a teenager myself and we were just making out and I repented for what I did. I was not an adult." Bishop D. said that didn't matter, I was an adult now and all your sins come back on you when you commit a similar sin, so he still considered me a child molester and he was writing a letter to the first presidency recommending I be excommunicated.

I felt like he was crazy and this was so unfair! I ended up writing a letter explaining what happened and sent it into the first presidency telling my side of the story. The church decided I was not an adult and I had repented for my sins and they allowed me to be sealed in the temple.

This was the first of many priesthood leaders that would judge me and make me feel unworthy and bad. Can you see the pattern? I couldn't at that time. The funny thing is now I see that it was myself creating this in others' behavior to validate what I already believed about myself. As a victim, I would blame them for judging me unfairly or un-righteously, things happened to me that was unfair. It wasn't my fault. I was misunderstood and wrongfully judged. I didn't understand that I created all of that with my core belief and that I was bad and a pervert. Once you understand we are creators and everything is about us, you can laugh at me as I do now. Oh my gosh, I am so cute! Look at me learning and making messes!

Chapter 9
Car crash and Scuba

It was December 1989. I was a cool 22 and I was married to Karri and had two boys. I was young and dumb and didn't listen to anything or anyone let alone God or the Spirit. I had taken a trip out to California with my best friend Mark Dodge. We were going scuba diving and had driven out in his car. He owned Wind and Wave a scuba diving shop next door to my photography studio. We became instant best friends.

We drove out to stay with one of Mark's friends named Mike. Mike was a teenage thirty-year-old. I thought Mark and Mike were old they were in their thirties! That was old. Now that I'm fifty-one, I have to laugh. That version of me would think I was a fossil. Mike loved to play but didn't care too much to grow up or embrace responsibilities. I thought he was super cool. He was a helicopter pilot and a scuba instructor but only worked when he wanted to. We all hit it off well and had a good time hanging out at his place and diving. Little did I know that on this trip I would almost die not once, but maybe three times? My angels would be working overtime to keep me alive.

Mark brayed his loud laugh and slapped me on the back, "This is going to be epic!" He said as we unloaded the scuba tanks form the back of Mike's car. We were preparing to go on a scuba diving trip off the coast of California. It was a shore dive where we entered the water from the shore and we were going to harvest or hunt some lobsters.

"Your first bug hunt! I bet you'll piss your wetsuit when you stick your arm into the hole and try and grab the ugly bugger." He laughed again braying like a donkey until tears were streaming from his eyes."I can't wait to see your half-hearted attempts to grab one!"

I remembered feeling defiant, I was a firefighter, I was not going to be scared of a lobster. That was just ridiculous. I was more than a little irritated with my best friend and scuba diving partner.

We were staying with Mark's buddy Mike who was also a scuba instructor who lived near the beach. Mike had taken us to a spot on the beach where we could find some nice lobsters on a nighttime dive. I was a fairly new scuba diver and just got my open water certificate.

I was feeling a little nervous about breaking the rules, but I was with two diving instructors. What could go wrong? It was a night dive. I had only done one other night dive before, and now Mike informed us that we are going to split up and dive separately. It was drilled into my head to always dive with a buddy you never dive alone. Mike reasoned we were all good divers and we could cover more ground and find more lobsters, so I didn't look like a wimp; I agreed it was a good idea.

We finally got the dive gear unloaded and carried it from the car down to the beach. We started to suit up when I felt the scampering animal of panic running in my chest clawing its way to freedom. The panic almost overwhelmed me. I took a staggering step and sat down hard on the beach. Mark was about fifteen feet away asked me, "Hey are you OK?"

I remember mustering my courage and saying, "Yeah, I just lost my balance." And a laughed a nervous little bark. Mark just shook his head and shouted, "Rookies!" I finished getting my wetsuit on and Mark came over and I helped put on his tank and BCD then he turned around and helped me do the same. I had forgotten how heavy and cumbersome the full gear and wetsuit was. I could barely move and walking in the sand and the waves were near impossible.

When I finally sunk into the inky black water and the weight was off me I felt incredibly free. The breaker waves were over four foot high and about impossible to swim through without getting tumbled like being in a washing machine. We submerged well before the waves broke and swam under that incredible power and weight of crushing water out into the black unknown. The only thing you could see is what your little dive light illuminated in front of you. Images of large sharks and sea monsters stalking you from behind were banished with admonishments and insults of being a little child of the opposite sex. It was an effort to control my breathing and remain calm. The unknown seems to hold the most fear in our lives. Not knowing what is going to happen especially when entering a dangerous situation that you know you could be killed. Knowing you had to trust your own wits, strength and trust the guys you are with to keep you safe was constantly on my mind as I swam toward the reef.

We had to swim out about three hundred yards to get to the rock formations where the lobsters lived. We stayed together at first and Mark showed me how to how to spot the lobsters antenna poking out of a hole at the base of the rocks and how you grabbed at them lightning fast grabbing the body part of the lobster and tried not to pull their antennas off. They would fight and try to wrap their spider-like legs around you and push off and swim away with their amazingly strong tail.

I watched Mark grab lobster after lobster with ease and dexterity. I swam away to another rock formation to try my own luck. I found a very small cave under a huge rock the size of a bus. I stuck my head into the hole and started to shine my flashlight around the large cavern looking for signs of lobsters. I swung the light from left to right and as I turned toward the right side of the cave I saw teeth.

Teeth, many, many, teeth stared at me opening and closing about 6 inches away from my face. I let out a bubbling scream as I backpedaled away from the cave. A moray eel swam out of the darkness. The eel's body must have been over four feet long and bigger around than a man's arm.

I swam over to Mark to show him my incredible find. I was excited and awed to see such an amazing creature and just a little scared. I motioned for him to come and see what I found. I pointed to the hole in the rock and tried to sign that an eel was in there. Mark stuck his head in the hole pulled it back quick reached in his mesh game bag and pulled out a lobster tail. He broke off a small chunk of meat and fed it to the eel-like someone would feed their pet dog. I was in awe of my friend. He was grinning like a kid through his mask at me. This was his element. I will always remember my good friend that way.

We separated and he swam off to collect more "bugs" I still had my first to catch. I am glad I was alone and not being witnessed at my pathetic attempts to grab at the underwater spiders in the holes. I don't think I even came close to grabbing one. Mark was right I would reach out try and grab one and feel them buck and grab at me and I would let go and snatch my hand back. I let out a sigh, "Maybe I am a little girl."

I swam from reef to reef looking for lobsters absorbed in the dive. I didn't want to come back and face the guys without one. I don't know how long I had been diving; I didn't check my watch or the air pressure gage for some time but when I finally did I only had five hundred pounds of air left. You start out with three thousand and at five hundred you must surface. I was surprised at how much air I had used. I looked around trying to see which way was back to shore. I couldn't tell so I decided to surface and see if I could see lights on the shore.

I was about thirty-five feet underwater and I slowly made my ascent. My head popped above the water's surface and I looked around. I shut off my dive light and let my eyes adjust to the darkness. I could see nothing but water and blackness. I spun in a circle scanning for any far-off lights to give me a clue as to which way shore was. I couldn't see any lights just wave after wave bouncing me like a cork in the blackness.

I yelled for my friends, "MIKE! MARK!!!! HEY!!! ANYONE!!! The only answer was the splashing of the water as the waves made me rise and fall. That little animal of panic started to run around in my chest again clawing for a way out. I was far offshore. How far did I swim?? I tried to tell which way the waves were traveling but I couldn't tell, they seemed to come from everywhere.

I pulled up my regulator with my air gauge and my compass on it. I knew east would lead me to shore. I turned on my dive light and leveled the gage in the water. The compass was dry and stuck in one position. I tried to tap it and get the needle to point north, and then I remembered Mark saying one of the regs had a broken compass. I guess I was the lucky one who got it. Crap!

Why did I swim so far? I shinned my dive light toward shore in hopes of seeing the reflection off the tail lights of the car, nothing only waves and blackness in every direction. I knew with my BCD I could float for hours and with my wetsuit, I could stay warm for hours but I knew my friends would start to worry about me and I didn't want to cause a fuss or have search and rescue called out because of me.

I closed my eyes and said a prayer, "Father, I'm lost I don't know which way shore is and I am scared. Please help me find which way shore is please help me." I prayed over and over.

I finally opened my eyes and looked around, still, nothing but blackness met my gaze.
I closed my eyes and tried to feel which way shore was, I spun my body in a circle searching for the feeling that would tell me which was the right. I felt calm one direction and I started to swim that way. I swam for about five minutes and stopped for a rest. I looked toward the way I was swimming and I thought I saw red brake lights light up in front and slightly left of me. Joy soared in my heart! I felt confirmation that I was going in the right direction.

I started to swim that way again with a little more energy and hope when I swam into the kelp forest. Scuba divers are warned to swim under the kelp and not try to get entangled in the long ropes of kelp that are thick over the surface. I instantly became entangled in the kelp not able to move forward or back. I pulled out my dive knife and began to cut myself free of the kelp.

I knew I needed to dive and swim under the kelp. I put the regulator in my mouth and let the air out of my BCD. I sank into the dark water and turned on my dive light. I tried to stay oriented in the direction I needed to swim. I descended to about ten feet above the bottom and started to swim toward shore. I had been swimming for about three minutes when it started to become more difficult to suck the air in. I looked at my air gauge and it was in the red.

I swam and breathed until I couldn't pull air into my lungs when I breathed in it just stopped and I knew I needed to surface. I ascended for the surface slowly letting air out of my lungs as I rose. I tried to not rise faster than the slowest bubbles. It felt like the surface was hundreds of feet above my head, not a mere twenty. My lungs burned as I neared the surface. My head popped out of the water my lungs screaming for air and took in a breath a little too early and got a mouth full of seawater. I coughed and choked and sucked in gasps of air in between coughs.

I finally got my breath and looked around. I was in open water I could see the waves breaking toward the shore a couple hundred yards in front of me, but I was still in the kelp forest. I had to inflate my BCD manually by blowing into the mouthpiece and holding the release button down. I inflated it fully so I was floating comfortably and tried to swim around the worst areas of the kelp. It was very tiring and slow going. I was constantly cutting myself free of the slimy ropes and I would move forward fighting for every foot I gained toward shore.

I was getting to the point of exhaustion where my arms and legs felt like lead. I would stop float and breathe, but I was becoming more and more fatigued with every foot I gained toward shore. "If I can just make it out of the kelp I will be fine." I kept saying to myself as I moved slowly forward.

When I finally made it out of the kelp forest I was so relieved to think my peril was behind me. I was coming up on the big waves called breakers that I would normally swim under but I had to surf in tonight. I felt the waves building and sucking me forward as I swam trying to stay ahead of the crushing water. My strength was depleted but I gave my last effort to out swim the wave. The water crashed into me pushing me toward the bottom and holding me there again I felt the sensation of drowning my lungs crying for oxygen. My BCD was fully inflated and I popped out of the waves grasp like a cork and bobbed while being propelled forward at a very fast speed with the waves.

I was being pushed by these large waves toward shore at an uncanny speed. I thought this is awesome I won't have to swim so far when I noticed I was being pushed to a jagged rock outcropping that the waves were smashing into with a violent explosion of the surf. I started to kick with my flippers on my back for all I was worth. I kicked and kicked by the rocks were rushing up to meet me with a crushing embrace. I knew I was not going to escape being slammed into the rocks. I mustered every ounce of strength I had left and kicked with all my might hoping to escape the rocks.

I was almost to them being propelled by a huge wave that crashed behind me and I braced for impact but incredibly the large rocks passed by on my right as I barely missed them and was swept past only to bounce my tank off some of the smaller rocks. The force that I hit the smaller rocks with dented the tank and slammed my teeth together biting into my tongue. Blood filled my mouth and my eyes saw stars or maybe that was because I was looking up into the night sky thanking God that I survived the worst of this night.

I was almost to shore when I tried to stand up but the waves took my legs out and I fell down into the water again. I was so shaky and had no strength left. I swam crawled up to the beach, but I couldn't crawl out of the surf. I just didn't have enough strength left. I lay half in half out of the water trying to breathe. When the waves covered me I would hold my breath underwater and when they pulled back I gulped the air in gasps.

It took me probably about ten minutes to recover enough that I could crawl out on the beach. I looked to my left and saw headlights coming toward me in the distance. I waved and was relieved to see Mike's car pulling up. Mark jumped out and gave me a hard time about going so far away from the group and how dangerous it was. I just smiled and nodded. Danger I understood.

Chapter 10
Party time.

The next night Mark and Mike wanted to go to the strip clubs. I was barely old enough to go and it was new to me so I agreed with all the enthusiasm my hormone driven body could muster. So we went out on the town to paint it red and set it on fire. We went from club to club drinking like fish. I can't remember if it was just one of us, or all of us that was puking in a dumpster behind one of the clubs then we all went back in and started drinking again.

I don't remember much of that night except the drive home that is seared into my memory. We were too drunk to stand up but Mike seemed to think it was ok to drive home. He couldn't walk in a straight line or stand without swaying but hey he could drive like a champ. I just cringe every time I think of that night. We should have killed ourselves and possibly some innocent people as well. I got into the back seat of Mike's Acura Legend. Mark was in the passenger seat and Mike was driving.

Somewhere along the way home, a police car tried to pull us over. Instead of complying he stepped on the gas pedal. We were racing through the streets of LA with a bunch of red and blue lights chasing us. That Acura was fast. We completely outran every one of those police cars. We were doing 130 mph through the city streets at 3 am. Red lights looked more like streaks as we blew through intersections.

I actually started crying and begging Mike to pull over I would get into the driver's seat and say I was driving. I would take the ticket for driving intoxicated. We were going to kill someone or our self. Mark and Mike just laughed at me and called me names that challenged my manhood. I shut up and just kept praying we would make it home safe.

Mike was going through a subdivision turning here and there he drove fast past his place and opened the garage door with the remote and we kept driving. He turned right and left and let the cops chase us another ten minutes. He then drove past his house again and pulled fast into the garage jumped out pulled the emergency release on the garage door and slammed it shut. I was still in the car trying to get out when I saw the red and blue lights pass the house searching for the Acura. They hadn't seen us pull in the garage or the door close. We got away with it, and I got teased for days for being scared in the back seat. I feel like 10,000 angels must have been along the route keeping everyone safe that crazy night. I still don't know how we made it home safe and not in jail or dead.

Chapter 11
Not listening to the spirit.

So you will probably understand why I didn't recognize the spirit when it warned me the next day. I wasn't really living my life in search of God. It's not the sin that keeps us from hearing God it's what we are tuned into. If we are constantly seeking God even when we are sinning we will hear Him and feel His love and answers. If we are caught up in just living our life for us and focused on things other than God, it's harder to hear Him when he tries to warn or help us.

Mike's sister was selling a 1983 5.0 Mustang it had only 15,000 miles on the engine and was in great shape for being 6 years old. Mike told me about this sweet car his sister had and I said I'll buy it. I was excited and said it with enthusiasm. I instantly heard a voice. It sounded in my head, "Do NOT buy that car". I shook my head and questioned; what? Why would I feel that way? I have the money. I can write a check for $3800 out of my account. I could get a loan on the car and put the money back into my business account when I got home. It was a good deal on the car she was selling it for low book. I could afford it and it was a car I wanted. I couldn't figure out what was wrong with the deal.

I pondered this cryptic message all afternoon and slowly began to reason and rationalize the feeling away. I had no idea that it was a message from an angel and from God. I thought it was just in my head. I wasn't in the habit of praying or asking God for answers let alone listening for them. Later that afternoon Mike was on the phone with his sister and he yelled at me, hey Ryan, are you still going to buy my sister's car? I yelled back hell yes!

DO NOT BUY THAT CAR shouted in my head again. I shook my head and was actually stunned. I remember feeling confused and a little scared. I had the feeling of impending doom come over me and I felt my heart race and flutter in my chest. I couldn't believe what I was feeling. I couldn't understand what it was a bad idea to buy the car? I spent the next few hours talking over the deal with myself. I was finally convinced that it was all in my head and I was going crazy when we drove over to Mike's sister's house to look at the car and buy it.

Mind you I hadn't even seen the car. I was so spontaneous. I was buying it sight unseen. We showed up at her house looked at the car loved it and I filled the check out. I went to hand her the check and the voice shouted three times louder than it had before. It was so loud I jerked the check back out of her hands and looked at her with this surprised look on my face. She was looking at me as if I was from Mars. I must have looked like a crazy man. I shook my head and realized how she was looking at me. I felt embarrassed and self-conscious so I shook off the feeling and handed her the check back. She said thank you and handed me the keys. I didn't feel the feeling again.

I went out to my new car beaming with pride. She was black and beautiful, with T-tops and a 5.0-liter engine. She roared when I started her up. She had a good sound system. The only thing I found to be wrong with her was the driver's seat belt didn't work. I tried sliding the metal tab into the buckle but it wouldn't latch. I messed with it and couldn't get it to work. I asked Mike about it and he said that it didn't work but I could pick one up from the junkyard cheap when I got home. They had disabled the warning light and the alarm so that wouldn't go off. I said Ok and we drove it back to Mike's place. We loaded up our bags and headed out to drive back to Utah.

It was the first of January, and I needed to be home on the second of January to shoot a wedding. I called my wife and told her I bought a new car. She said, "what"? I said, "I mean I bought you a new car. I will probably still drive our pickup truck." She was ok with that and asked if I would be home on time to shoot the wedding and I said yes we were just leaving.

By the time we got on the road, it was almost 11 pm. We rolled into Vegas at 3:45 am. I stopped the car and Mark pulled up beside me in his car. I told him I needed to get a hotel and sleep for a few hours. I couldn't keep my eyes open. He said no way. He wanted to drive to Wendover, which was at the top of the state of Nevada. We would have to go up I-93 through the middle of nothing but desert and sagebrush to go to Wendover and it was hundreds of miles out of our way. I complained there was no way. Why did he want to go up there? He reminded me of the girl we met on the way out we had driven through Wendover and stayed at the hotel-casino. She worked there as a waitress and Mark had struck up a conversation with her. He wanted to go see if he could get her number.

I told him I know I can't drive that far and stay awake, he said don't be such a pussy, roll down your windows rub snow in your face, turn your music up you can do this. I reluctantly succumbed to his request and we headed up I-93 toward my doom. I caught myself falling asleep and so I slapped my face hard enough to leave a red mark. It woke me up for a few minutes. I had the windows down and the January winter air was blasting into the car. It was so cold I was shivering. I was screaming along with the hard rock music I was listening to. I was doing everything I could to stay awake. And it worked at least for a hundred and fifty miles.

About 100 miles outside of Ely Nevada I fell asleep. My eyes were open but I just zoned out. The road turned to the right but the car kept going straight about 70 mph. I woke up off the road in deep snow the car bouncing over uneven ground. I hit a few hard jolts and then hit an embankment and the car went airborne. I flew through the air for what seemed like a long time but in reality was probably pretty short. I came down on the nose of the car and folded the car in half. The seat broke off the track the T-tops shattered the steering wheel broke and the wind was knocked out of me. I didn't know it but I had broken my back at t-11 and had ruptured 5 discs in my back. My intestines were also bleeding.

 I was trying to breathe but I couldn't get my lungs to inflate. I was in so much pain and I was on the point of panic when Mark showed up at the car. He had seen me leave the road and had been honking his horn to wake me up. He stopped his car and ran across the snow-covered ground about two hundred yards to where I had crashed my new car. He asked me if I was ok, but I couldn't talk I just shook my head and mouthed can't breathe. He said don't worry the wind is just knocked out of you. He tried to open my door but it was jammed tight and wouldn't open. He tried pulling me out but, get this, my seatbelt was on.

My seatbelt was on! How in the world did it get on me and latch into the buckle? We had tried it and it wouldn't work. Mark reached across me and tried to unbuckle the seat belt but he couldn't get it to release. He pulled out his pocket knife and cut the seatbelt. He reached in and pulled me out the window. As he pulled me out pain as I've never experienced before shot up and down my back. It was so bad I passed out as he carried me across the snow to his car. I woke up as he was putting me into his car. He drove me the 100 miles to Ely to the first hospital we came to. I kind of faded in and out of consciousness on the way to the hospital. I don't remember most of the drive.

They x-rayed me and told me I had broken T-11 they didn't have an MRI so the recommended I go to the hospital when I got home. They didn't have the equipment to properly diagnose me. So they offered to transport me by ambulance to a hospital in Utah. I figured that would be very expensive and I didn't know if my car insurance would cover anything so I declined. They gave me pain medication and helped put me in Mark's car. They didn't even put me on a backboard but just doped me up and put me in Mark's car. He drove me the 400 miles to home.

When I got home I went to another hospital and they did an MRI and told me that I had broken T-11 and I was within 1/16 of an inch from severing my spinal cord. The physician just shook his head with amazement when he heard how Mark had pulled me from the car. He couldn't understand how I was not paralyzed, and the fact the other hospital didn't put me on a backboard for transport. He was amazed I made it through all of that without severing the cord. After they treated me and sent me home to heal on my back for the next six weeks, I eventually healed but I would never be the same.

God had spared my life and kept me from being paralyzed but I would end up having two more back surgeries and a lot of therapy to get where I wasn't in constant pain. Now when I hear the promptings of the spirit I listen and listen quick.

Chapter 12
Plane (almost) Crash

I was a young man of twenty-three, married and we had two boys. Sean was my oldest and was four, and Brandon was two and a half. My father was an airline pilot and so was my older brother. My Dad flew for Frontier Airlines and Continental Airlines, and my brother flew for United.

I wanted to be a pilot so I was working toward getting my license. I had been flying off and on since I was sixteen working toward my certificate. I had to fly a cross-country flight over one hundred and fifty nautical miles with full-stop landings at three locations. I was flying from Ogden Airport to St. George. My friend Greg lived in St. George was also a pilot. I was flying down to have lunch with him and his wife. We planned on spending the night with them and flying back the next day.

Solo cross-country means the pilot must be alone and have no passengers in the plane. I being an arrogant twenty-four year old decided that I would take my wife and my two young children, Sean who was five, and Brandon who was three with me. I reasoned even though I wasn't supposed to I had a lot of experience flying since I had been working on it since I was 16. I loaded everyone into the plane in Ogden and took off on a beautiful November morning. The weather was clear not too cold and the sun was shining. We had a nice flight and made a landing in Cedar City to meet the requirements and took off again for St. George.

We landed in St. George and were met by Greg and his wife and we went to a restaurant and ate. Greg asked me if I had looked at the weather report and I said no. He informed me that a big storm was going to move in up north and maybe I had better head back tonight and beat the storm. If the storm were bad I would be stuck down there in St. George for a couple of days waited for it to clear. I needed to get back to work on Monday and felt like I couldn't take a chance on missing work.

We headed back to the airport and went into the flight office to amend my flight plan. I looked at the weather and later that evening a big storm was moving in bringing snow and poor visibility. If I didn't get out now I probably would be stuck a couple of days.

It was about four o'clock in the afternoon and we started prepping the plane for the flight home. I did my pre-flight walk around and checked the oil and gas levels and made sure the plane was in good visual condition. It looked good and so we loaded everyone on board and started the engine. I ran through my checklist and listened to the current conditions. I set my altimeter and informed the tower that I was ready with information "Foxtrot". Information Foxtrot is the phonetic alphabet designation for the weather information given for the particular hour. It changes to the next letter when that hour is up, so after "Foxtrot" would be information "Golf". When you inform the tower you have that information lets them know you have set your altimeter to the correct settings and you know the current weather conditions.

I was cleared for takeoff and the Cessna 182 Skylane roared into the sky. The powerful Lycoming 6 cylinder engine made the little plane feel more like a sports car on the sunny November afternoon. I loved flying; the feeling of freedom surged through my veins. I felt powerful and free. I tuned the radio to the first beacon we were to fly to. Back then way before GPS, we flew from radio beacon to radio beacon and that's how you navigated across the country.

As I passed Cedar City the sun was beginning to set. A beautiful sunset painted the mountains and landscape far below me. I enjoyed the beauty of God's creation below me. It was the last good feeling I was to have for a while. The sky darkened. I was beginning to get a little concerned when it got full dark. I had flown a few times at night, but it was always completely different than flying during the day. You rely on instruments and on direction, altitude, and airspeed more than you do on what you can see to fly toward. It's kind of like driving at night and shutting the lights off. You get the feeling of not knowing what is in front of you.

I relied on the instruments and flew from beacon to beacon at the correct altitude. I was flying a northeast direction so I was flying at an odd elevation plus five hundred feet. I was at 11,500 feet to be above any mountains and along the correct flight lane and altitude to avoid other aircraft. I was flying at about 120 knots and the air was smooth without any turbulence. I started to settle into a rhythm I wasn't feeling as nervous this night flying wasn't so bad.

I got over the Fairfield VOR or radio beacon and noticed some clouds off to the port side of the aircraft. As I flew further north the clouds moved in closer and closer. I was flying along about 25 miles south of Antelope Island when everything went black and I was in the middle of a cloud. I couldn't see anything outside of the airplane. I knew I had to get out of the cloud as soon as I could so I started dropping altitude. I pushed the yoke forward and watched the altimeter tell me I was dropping about 800 feet per minute I broke out of the clouds and could see about 1000 feet lower, I continued on down to 9,500 feet above sea level so I would still be at the correct altitude. I figured I dropped 2000 feet I would be safe and stay out of the clouds. I pulled out my map and looked at where I was and the elevations of the surrounding mountains. I was above everything around me so I felt like I was going to be fine.

I continued to head toward Ogden. I would be flying past the west side of Antelope Island. I was looking out to the west and could see a huge storm front moving in. I kept scanning the sky for clouds but it was hard to see in the dark. Suddenly everything went black again and I knew I was in the clouds. I started to drop altitude and keep looking outside the window for a break in the clouds. I began to develop what's called spatial disorientation or vertigo. The signals my body was giving me were different than the actual position of the aircraft. I felt like I was flying straight and level but when I looked at the instruments it showed an angle to my wings like I was in a turn. I turned the airplane the opposite way to correct it and the angle became worse instead of better. I looked at the altimeter and it said I was loosing 1500 feet a minute more than I thought so I pulled back on the yoke to slow my descent. It became worse and increased up to 2000. I thought something must be wrong with the plane's instruments and I tapped them with my finger just in case they were stuck in a vacuum or something. It just didn't make sense. I couldn't see anything and everything I did was backward.

That's when God spoke to me. Well boomed at me is more accurate. I heard in a voice as loud as thunder PUSH DOWN AND TURN RIGHT! I thought that doesn't make sense. It came even louder if possible so I did what I was told I pushed on the yoke and turned right.

The plane was upside down. As I began my descent and I was looking out the window one of the wings dropped I rolled the plane over and didn't even know it because being in a dive simulated gravity and kept us glued to our seats. So being upside down everything I did to correct what the instruments were telling me made the situation worse. I was upside down headed toward the peak of Antelope Island. As I tried to pull up on the yoke it took me faster toward the ground. I was flying right into the mountain at 140 knots per hour.

When God told me to push down and turn right it rolled the plane out of being inverted into an upright position. I broke out of the clouds but my brain couldn't process what I was seeing for a couple of seconds. I thought I was going to hit a big military airplane like a C-135 out of HAFB but it was the peak of the Island with the lights of the city behind it. I realize I was about three seconds away from becoming a huge fireball on the side of the mountain. I pulled back on the yoke with all my might. We pulled at least a couple of "G" forces as we were driven into our seats. It woke everyone up in the airplane as the plane pulled out of the dive and barely missed hitting the ground by a hundred yards.

My wife had been asleep and woke up in a panic asking if we were ok. We are fine, I lied, I just had to pull up to avoid some clouds. She said ok and went back to sleep. My heart was slamming in my chest and I was shaking like a leaf in a hurricane. I wiped the sweat off my forehead and headed away from the Island out into the middle of the Great Salt Lake. The wind was blowing so hard that I could see huge whitecaps on the surface of the lake as I skimmed above the lake at about 500 feet off the ground. I had to stay low to stay out of the clouds. I took a few deeps breaths and settled myself down. I turned the plane to the Ogden VOR and starting flying toward the airport.

The wind was blowing in gusts from the west. I was flying toward the airport, which was uncontrolled at this time of night, which meant there wasn't anyone in the tower working as air traffic control. As I got close to the airport runway I could click my mike three times on the frequency of the tower and it would turn on the lights for the runway. I lined up with runway 36 and turned on the lights. The wind was blowing so hard from the west that it made the plane fly at an angle or crabbed into the wind to fly straight. I had practiced crosswind landings before with my flight instructor but the biggest wind I had landed in was seven knots. The wind was blowing about 20 knots and gusting to 40 to 50 knots.

I was so crabbed into the wind that when I was flying straight down the runway I was almost sideways. As the plane got close to the runway I would kick in opposite rudder and bring the tail in alignment with the runway. This caused the wings to be unleveled and one tire would touch down first. Just as my tire touched the runway a big gust of wind hit the airplane and blew me off the runway. I quickly added power and flew the plane back to the center of the runway. I tried landing again. Before the tire even got close to the runway another gust blew me off into the dirt again.

I added power and flew the plane back to the center of the runway a second time and realized I was quickly running out of runway. I had to get the plane down this time or I may not be able to safely land. I lined up kicked in rudder but instead of pulling the power this time I kept the power on to combat the wind and forced the plane to the ground with the power on. As soon as the wheels touched down I pulled power and pushed the yoke forward to keep the plane on the ground. I hit the brakes and watched the plane slow and stop just at the end of the runway. I had less than twenty feet left before I would have ended up in the dirt.

I turned the plane around and taxied to my hanger. Once I got in front of my hanger and shut the plane down I started crying. I shook and shook and cried my eyes out. My wife was wondering what was wrong with me. Why I was so upset. I couldn't talk for a while and finally managed to say I almost killed us. She helped get me out of the plane and push it back into the hanger. She had to drive our car home because I couldn't drive. I was so shaken up. I had almost killed my entire family not once but twice.

God was keeping me around for a reason. I just didn't know what that reason was. Nor would I time after time He saved my bacon I couldn't understand why he would save a sinner such as me.

Chapter 13
Firefighter

One of the best parts of my life and the part I started to feel manlier was when I became a firefighter. I started off as a volunteer for Syracuse City in 1991. I wore a pager and I would respond to the station when an emergency was paged out. I quickly fell in love with the adrenaline of the job.

I became an Emergency Medical Technician and got my other certifications. I applied for a bigger department that had the possibility of going full time. Layton City was a great department to work for. We had an ambulance service and I was able to work twenty-four-hour shifts and stay at the fire station.

I so desperately wanted to fit in and be accepted by the other men. I always felt small and weak. I had been working as a photographer for years and loved art, classical music, and the ballet. I was so afraid that I was nothing like the other firefighters who worked construction and other manly jobs. They all seemed so different than the sensitive artistic young man that I was. I hated it. I wanted to be different than I was. I wanted to be tough, rugged, and a man that other men looked up to.

One morning I got to the station to work a twenty-four-hour shift starting at seven. The crew that was just getting off shift was standing around the ambulance and talking with the crew coming on to shift, which I was among them. One of the full-time firefighters who was getting off shift was a guy who rode bulls in the rodeo and laid carpet when he wasn't putting out fires. He was a big tough cowboy who sported a big handlebar mustache.

He had shaved it off. Everyone was shocked at his appearance. He had worn that mustache for years. It just didn't look like him without it. One of the firefighters commented that he looked younger, one laughed about his baby face, one said that his face looked naked.

To my horror, I found myself commenting, "I think it brings out the blue in your eyes." What did I just say? My mind screamed at me to take it back, or say something to make it funny. All around me the other eight men looked at me with their mouths agape. No one said anything for a few seconds until one cracked a joke by saying, "Big Boy." He said it in a sexy voice and batted his eyes. I wanted to crawl into a hole and die! I was mortified. Here I was trying to fit in and be "one of the guys", and instead I alienate them all with my stupid comment. Good lord here I was trying to impress them as being part of the group and now I put my foot in my mouth.

I never did overcome that day and I never quite fit in from that point on. The poor guy I made the comment about started to get called "Ol' Blue Eyes" by the other guys. I'm sure he hated me from that day on. I ended up getting an award at the Christmas party that year. The award was for "Actions Unbecoming of a Firefighter" and the story was told to the whole department and their families while Ol' Blue Eyes and I stood at the front of the room as the Assistant Chief tried to tell the story. He was laughing so hard he was wheezing and couldn't get the story out. Blue Eyes just glared at me daggers of ice...., blue ice to be exact.

I don't think I have ever been more embarrassed. The funny thing is when I have run into those guys recently they marvel at how muscular and big I have gotten, they look at me with my tattoos and huge muscles and say they would never have recognized me they still thought of me as the scrawny firefighter who made embarrassing comments.

Chapter 14
Flashover

I got hired as a full-time firefighter for Murray City a few years later. I remember a five-alarm fire at a restaurant supply company one night; we were part of the mutual aid as the business was in a neighboring city. I had never seen a fire so big. Propane gas canisters would "pop off" with explosions that sounded like cannon fire one after another all night long. It sounded like the biggest string of firecrackers in the world.

I was awed and amazed at the power and rage of a fire that big, but that was not nearly as impressive as being in the belly of the beast or inside a house fire spraying water while the fire raged over and around you.

I was a fairly new rookie firefighter when the alarm went off at station 82 in Murray. We ran to the fire truck and were first on the scene. I jumped off the truck as a mother ran from the house and grabbed me by the arm. Smoke poured out of the front door of the house and you could see flames in the windows. The rush hit me. The mother was screaming hysterically, "My son is in there!" over and over as she pulled me toward the house. My training told me to suppress the fire first and search for victims second. I knew the next truck on the scene would be the rescue truck and would go in and search for the boy after we knocked the fire down.

Even though I knew better I followed the Mom to the front door I had my SCBA or self-contained breathing apparatus on and was breathing canned air so the smoke didn't bother me, but as I stepped into the house and yelled for her son, I couldn't even see an inch in front of my face the smoke was so thick. I knew it was useless to search for her son until the fire was knocked down. I remembered the kids we lost in Layton and didn't want to lose this boy. I was going to do anything I could to save him.

I ran back out of the house and my captain was doing my job in my absence. He had pulled the hose off the truck and shouldered the hose bundle as he started to advance toward the house. He saw me and gave me the hose. We went through the front door of a split level house and headed down the "chimney" of the fire. Because the fire was in the basement the heat and smoke were coming up the basement stairs and exiting out the front door. Even with our fire "turnouts" or protective gear that was fire and heat resistant on it felt like a blowtorch on my face and hands. The flames rolled over our heads across the ceiling. I don't think I have ever seen anything so beautiful or terrifying as a whole room on fire with flames rolling like waves across everything around you.

I opened up the nozzle and started spraying water on the fire. "Put the wet stuff on the red stuff" was the simple way to explain our job. Water expands over seventeen hundred times in size when it turns to steam. The water hit the fire and instantly turned to hot steam. Dry heat doesn't burn anything on your skin as bad as wet heat. The superheated steam hit us and made the captain and I curl into a ball holding the hose as we hunkered down praying the fire would die and we would live. Pain like someone holding a hot curling iron against my face and hands made me want to panic and run out of the house.

To exit, I would have to climb over my captain and I would be forever shamed as the rookie who couldn't handle the heat. I just hunkered lower moving the hose from side to side and praying that we would make it out of there alive. One of the other rooms reached a flash point and we experienced a flashover where everything in the room reaches ignition temperature at once and instantly explodes in flames and hot gasses. You might have heard about a backdraft which is similar, a backdraft is where everything is at ignition temperature but the oxygen has been burnt up. When oxygen is reintroduced everything explodes into flames. These are some of the most dangerous conditions a firefighter has to battle.

I was sure we were dead when that happened. It was so hot before I couldn't even understand how hot it instantly it became. My mind couldn't process how bad or dangerous the situation was. I only know I was gripped in complete panic. I felt my captain reach over me and turn the nozzle's adjustment from the spray pattern to fog. That sprays the water in a wide fog and creates a cool zone around the firefighters. It instantly cooled down like a thousand degrees we went from the surface of the sun to mercury. Still so hot you couldn't stand it but not hot enough to melt my brain.

We vacillated between fog and stream hitting the fire and then fogging us to cool things down. I was so grateful for an experienced captain. Gil Rodriguez was the best. He saved us. We were able to knock the fire completely down so the rescue crew could come in and find the boy. He was a mentally disabled boy who had been playing with fire in his room. When the fire got out of control he panicked. He was afraid he was going to get into trouble so he hid under the bed instead of running out of the house. That is where the other crew found him. He was unconscious and not breathing. They took him out and paramedics revived him and took him to the hospital.

Two weeks later the boy and his mother came to the station and made us a cake and thanked us for saving his life. It was one of the best moments of my job. I went through something incredibly hard that I didn't think I would make it out of and ended up doing something good for someone else and making a difference. How many times have we had something happen in our lives or you have seen others go through something that was hard and when it's over the joy and satisfaction floods in. You don't have to fight a dragon or put out a fire and save a little boy's life to be a hero. Sometimes saying something kind to a person struggling with depression is enough to save a life.

We can all be heroes and give of ourselves or go through something hard for someone else's benefit. I know I was protected that day. I imagine my angels had their wings spread over us protecting us from the heat and saved our lives.

A few years later a good friend of mine that I went through rookie school with died while fighting a fire in similar conditions. The fire got too hot and they exited the building but because it was so hot my friend Kendal got turned around and went deeper into the house instead of following the hose out with the rest of the crew. I often think about how close Gil and I came that day to have the same thing happen. I know it was just another time I had been saved by God for a greater purpose.

Even though I was protected and preserved by God didn't mean my life was easy. If my wife and I weren't struggling financially we were fighting. The marriage was challenging all the time and neither one of us were even aware of how to fix what was wrong.

We had no skills, no communication skills, no skills to even try and understand ourselves, or improve. We were just acting out our programming. And when you have two people acting out their programming with a painful background it is a perfect recipe for drama. We constantly fought and acted out our pain. We figured if we quit sinning and making mistakes that God would fix our marriage. We tried so hard to get worthy and change our behaviors so that we could go to the temple and get sealed as a family for time and all eternity. It was kind of like putting a new paint job on a car and expecting it to run better.

We finally made it after three years of working hard and got sealed in the summer of 2000. All my marital problems were over. Hooray! I finally made it to happiness. Yeah... that lasted about six months. By January the next year, I found out that my wife was having an affair with her another man I was devastated. I had sacrificed so much and worked so hard to fix things, how could they fall apart at the finish line? She wasn't willing to quit seeing him and we divorced a few months later. They moved in together and about a year later she married him.

I want to add what an amazing person she is and how much I love and respect her to this day. We have lessons in life that are perfect for us and what we create. I made my mistakes too and did things to cause her to feel like she had no choice but to do what she did. I honor her and thank her for all the lessons I learned from her and what an amazing spirit she has and what a good mom she has been to our children. I would never want to say anything to hurt her but our experiences helped shape my life which I get to share with you.

I loved it when God shows me this part of my life when I was having my NDE and I saw this through His eyes. (A little bit of foreshadowing)

Chapter 15
Near Death Experience

March 11th, 2001.
I had escaped death many, many times. God has always miraculously saved me so I was not worried. I was in a safe place, my photography studio, no one ever died in there. I had just finished watching a movie with my family on the projector in my theater room where I showed clients images.

We had just got done watching Flash Gordon the 1980 cult classic starring Sam Jones. The movie credits were moving up the screen while Queen sang Flash Aaaaahhhaa he'll save every one of us, and the kids, Brandon, age 12, and his little sister, Alyssa, age 7 were dancing in the light singing along. My wife had taken the toddler, Alex, in the house to put him into bed and my oldest Sean age 14 was staying the night at a friend's house.

Earlier in the day I had tripped over a cord and pulled one of my studio flashes over and had broken the light, the flash tube, and the housing. I decided to look at the light and see if it could be fixed. The housing had broken out the electrical plug identical to what is in most computers, a three-prong male part that plugged into a female cord. The male part was connected to wires on the back that went to various circuit boards in the flash. I unplugged these wires and tried to pull the broken part off the electrical cord. I realized at this time that I needed to be careful; the light was still plugged into the electrical outlet.

I went over to where it was plugged in along with 3 other lights and unplugged the one I thought I was working on. I unplugged the wrong cord. I walked back to where I was working on the light, picked up the cord and tried again to pull the broken plastic piece off the electrical cord. It still wouldn't budge.

I consider myself to be a pretty smart guy, maybe even damn near a genius. In fact, my own brilliance surprises me sometimes. So in my brilliance, I decided to use my teeth as pliers and pull the broken part off the electrical cord!

The metal prongs touched my tongue as I bit down on the plastic part; electricity quickly grabbed and paralyzed me. I had never been so frozen into place, and I had been shocked before. The pain was unbearable. The electricity violently buzzed every cell of my body filling every cell with unbearable pain.

I tried to pull out the cord with all my strength. I strained and pulled but I couldn't make my muscles do anything but clench in complete rigidity. I tried to move my eyes away from the cord I was looking at, I wondered if my kids would see me and come to my rescue. I couldn't even move my eyes! I had no control over my body. The electricity controlled me making me dance to the funky chicken.

Funny thing was I was not really worried or concerned at this point. I figured the circuit breaker would pop or my kids would find me and unplug the cord. God had always saved me before out of situations much worse than this, seemingly impossible situations of impending death and doom were always remedied by that amazing God who seemed to care about me despite my imperfections.

I suddenly became concerned when smoke began to billow out of my mouth in little black puffs growing to a full steam coal-powered locomotive. I couldn't believe that much smoke was coming out of me! I was frying! I was cooking! Every cell felt like it was going to explode, even my brain was frozen making it hard to think. Then it hit me I knew this was it! I was going to die.

I was so disappointed. This is how I was going to die! Are you kidding me!! Thoughts swirled in my head about all the close calls I was saved from, my close calls or brushes with death. No, I couldn't have died in the near plane crash going out in a fireball, or in a car crash when I broke my back. I couldn't die in the house fire when everything exploded in flames at once when I was firefighter saving a little boys life, I couldn't die a hero. NOOO, I'm going to die from stupidity! I'm going to get a Darwin award. I'm going to be a joke on the Internet.

I was not really upset about dying but the manner of it and how I would look to others. This is a prime example of how much my ego ruled my life. It makes me laugh now.

A bright light appeared above my head. My body was frozen, my eyes couldn't move off the cord in my mouth, my heart couldn't beat, my brain could barely fire off a thought through the background static and buzz of the electricity, but I raised my view up into the light.

The light was the most beautiful awe-inspiring visual I had yet ever seen. I cannot put into words how it made me feel. I felt myself rising up toward the source of the light, floating about my body staring into the pure white light. The light enveloped me, caressed me, and a feeling of traveling or speed overcame me as I entered the light fully.

I appeared in a white room of the purest beautiful white I had ever seen. I feeling of excitement and anticipation grew in my breast until I could not hold it anymore and I found myself shouting for joy! I knew where I was and where I was going. I shouted over and over "yes!" My excitement and joy, I was going home to my Father!

I cannot compare the excitement I felt to any feeling I had ever had on earth. The only thing I could say is the excitement on Christmas morning when your parents said you could get up at 7:00 in the morning and it was 6:58 and you had only two more minutes to wait to experience the best morning of your life. Times that by a million and you might be close to what I felt.

God appeared behind a barrier of whiteness, like a curtain, but His radiance glowed a golden white so brilliant I could barely make out His form. It was like one of those huge Hollywood searchlights was pointed at me. My joy leaped in my breast. I was overcome and filled with love so poignant so encompassing as to erase any pain and sorrow life had up to that moment given me. The most heartbreaking pain I had felt and carried in my soul melted and was replaced with the most profound feeling of peace and everything was right and perfect.

I felt God's love that is beyond description. It was the most complete, whole and perfect I have ever felt. Just being in His presence was enough to change me forever. I cannot give you any earthly experience that is even close to what it feels like. There is no point of reference. It is like describing the taste of salt to someone who had never tasted salt. It is desirable above all else I have ever experienced.

I felt God's joy at seeing me. There was no disappointment or judgment that I could have done better or I was lacking, there was only a feeling of Him running toward me throwing His arms around my neck and crying with joy with his face buried into my neck, my son is home! Just like I imagine the father in the prodigal son.

I thought I would have so many questions and worries to ask God, why is there so much pain in life? Why do good people suffer? Why do those we love hurt us? Why am I not in trouble and being sent to hell? How can you forgive me when I have not even repented yet? I couldn't think of one concern when I was in heaven. It was like everything was perfect. I was just in awe and loving how it felt. I wish I would have asked a few questions now that I'm back in my body, but I guess I will have to get answers from God like the rest of us, faith and prayers.

God moved through the veil and stood in front of me. He showed me my life in detail every moment through His eyes of love. Nothing was left out. The good and the bad were shown without judgment. It all happened instantly while I was with God in the blink of an eye. I saw the bad things I had done, and the sins, but I felt no shame, no remorse only love for the lesson learned. I saw bad things are done to me that hurt me deeply, and I remember thinking, "Why was I so upset about that? It was such a beautiful lesson!" Everything in this life was there to help us learn and grow in love and forgiveness. Life was about learning not about a test you could fail. There was no failure, only lessons designed to teach us and help us teach others.

I understood little of what I saw except one thing God loved me regardless of what I had done that was wrong or bad. His love was unconditional. I was here to learn and grow from my experiences not to prove if I was worthy of His love or being able to return to Him. Everything I had been taught by religion about not being enough and having to earn my way home by being righteous didn't make sense. Our sins and sorrows were there to teach us, give us a point of reference, not qualify us for eternal life with Him. We could all come home. He had provided a way, and all we had to do was to accept it and love Him and want to be with Him. My understanding of this grew more and more over the years as the experience sank in along with other spiritual experiences.

I looked at God and His incredible brilliance and I felt so complete, so at home, nothing was missing in my life. I was bliss and one with God. I never wanted to leave that feeling. I had never been happier or felt more whole, in comparison life on earth, felt so alone and empty. I had done a lot of amazing and fun things on earth, I had traveled all over the world, scuba dived with sharks in Australia, skydived, bungee jumped off a bridge, I ran into burning buildings and saved people, I have made fortunes and lost them, I was a pilot and had taken a few aerobatic lessons, but nothing compared. Add everything fun and exciting I had ever done and it was nothing in comparison to how I felt in God's presence. It was so freaking amazing. I felt completely whole and nothing was lacking.

God asked me a question. "Do you want to come home with me, or do you want to go back to them?" and He waved his hand toward the floor. The floor I was standing on was pure white and it began to turn foggy and then was clear. I was standing in the air about 20 feet above my children. They were playing in the light of the projector as the movie had just ended. They were making shadow puppets and giggling to each other. They were completely unaware that their Dad was being electrocuted in the next room less than twenty feet away.

My heart sank. "They need me!" I cried out. My heart was breaking I didn't want to leave this feeling. I didn't want to go back, but they needed me! Oh, it was so hard to choose, incredible as that may sound, but it's true, I didn't want to leave God's presence even to be with my kids.

God said, "I will see you again," and in the blink of an eye I was back in my body. It was like getting hit by a truck! The electricity slammed me so hard and all of the pain returned. I thought in desperation, "Why would God send me back to my body, but not get me off of the electricity?" It's a good question, right? I felt totally justified in asking it.

God answered with, "Oh? Did you ask for help?"

Wow! I felt chagrinned. I kind of missed that part. I pleaded, "Heavenly Father please help!" and the cord moved as someone pulled it. I screamed holy crap in my mind and I started pulling with all my strength. God made me give everything I had to pull the cord out, but He made up the impossible part. I could have been the strongest man in the world and couldn't overcome my own muscles when they are frozen with electricity. Just like the atonement, He took the impossible part, the part I couldn't do and made up for my weakness. He set me free of what was binding me, both temporally and physically. He taught me a very valuable lesson as he saved my life.

It was such a beautiful lesson for me about the atonement. His love is perfect, unconditional, unwavering. He sees past our lessons, He knows us, and the major battles we chose to learn from in this life. He placed us into the conditions and situations in this life that would give us the greatest chance to learn, to choose to love ourselves in spite of our mistakes.

The atonement of Christ makes up the impossible part of overcoming our mistakes. It makes us whole even though we came to be broken, shattered, and unworthy. We do not know what's it like to be healthy until we are sick. We desperately wanted the opposition, the sin, the sorrows, and the mistakes; it was the only way we could learn what we chose to learn. But for us to learn these lessons would make us broken, shattered, and in a different state than we left heaven to come to earth.

We needed something beyond what we could do to overcome this, that is where Christ and the atonement come in to mend our broken heart, heal our shattered spirit, make us whole and complete again. The gift of grace is what we are given but we cannot earn, but that doesn't mean we have nothing to do. God wants us to give our maximum effort to overcome the things that are binding us, holding us back, and retarding our growth. Just like the electricity froze me and was destroying me, addictions and sin do that for our growth. But what is our maximum effort, the problem is we compare sins, we compare efforts, I am less righteous than someone else. I know I could have done better. I know I didn't give my best effort. We think those things and judge ourselves. When the only one who knows our best effort is God. Don't give up on yourself; don't judge yourself for being a failure, or not doing enough. Do your best, but if you fail, know that God has you.

We do our best to overcome, give forth our maximum effort to pull the cords out of our mouth, but many of us stay stuck. What is keeping you stuck? What is impeding your growth? What is the thing you are struggling with? Whatever it is, ask God for help while simultaneously forgiving yourself on a radical level, realize and know you are enough. Often it is our guilt and shame that keeps us stuck, let it go and let the peace flow in. If you do I promise you miracles will happen for you as it did for me.

The cord popped out of my mouth and my muscles went from being locked up and rigid to rubber. The electricity had kept my mind conscious even though my heart had not been beating for six minutes when the cord was plugged my vision and consciousness went out just like when a TV is unplugged. My vision started contracting into a pinpoint and then went black, I was not even aware that I had fallen face first into the floor.

My twelve-year-old son heard the crash from the other room and came running in to check on what happened. He saw his Dad laying face down on the floor. He ran to me grabbed me and rolled me over. I was unconscious and not breathing. He shook me in a panic calling "Dad!, Dad!, Dad!" over and over.

I took a breath as if swimming from a great depth to the surface of the water. My eyes popped open and my first sight was of my son covering his mouth with both hands and saying "Oh my gosh!" He let go of me and ran for the phone. He frantically called 911 and waited for the operator to answer the phone. I heard him say, "I found my Dad he was laying on the floor not breathing, I shook him and he took a breath. Black smoke came out of his mouth and his tongue looks all burnt!"

They took me to the hospital. I was exhausted and weak, but alive. I was back. My wife had our baby and two of my other three kids in the hospital room with me. I looked at them and wondered why I had felt so strongly that I had to come back. They would have been fine without me, I thought, why did I leave? Little did I know that in a few months my wife would leave me and the kids for her best friends husband and the world I knew would be turned upside down. My kids desperately needed me. I had a purpose I just didn't know it yet.

The physician on duty in the emergency room came in and examined me. I had burnt a hole through my tongue where the contacts from the electrical plug had touched it. It was about the size of a quarter and had burned the flesh to charcoal. It was crispy and crumbled to the touch. It had gotten so hot in my mouth that it had melted my silver fillings in my teeth. The lower teeth's fillings pooled silver and bright again instead of the normal almost black color. The top teeth fillings had melted and run out of the cavity holes.

The doctor told me he wasn't worried about my tongue, it would heal in a couple of weeks and all I would be left with is a scar. He also told me he wasn't worried about my teeth, my dentist could fix that, what he was worried about was organ damage. He informed me that 110-volt electricity cooks it's victims from the inside out like a microwave, while 220-volt electricity burns externally and blows off body parts. He said I was cooked on the inside. He was very worried I would go into organ failure overnight. He said given the damage in my mouth and the estimated time of six minutes it wasn't if I had organ damage but how much. He said my brain, heart, liver, kidneys, and on and on were damaged. He was going to run some enzyme tests, which would show what kind of damage and to what extent.

The next morning the nurse came in and disconnected my IV and took my tubes out. The Physician came in a few minutes later and told me that he had discharged me and I could go home. I was speechless. "Wait, What? I stammered, what about the organ damage? The doctor shook his head and said, "I ran the tests three times because I thought there must be an error in the test, but they came out negative for enzymes every time. There are no enzymes from organ damage in your blood. That is impossible given the damage to your mouth and the time you were being electrocuted. I am a man of science, not faith, but you are a miracle. Go home and count yourself lucky."

I was shocked. Ok bad pun, but this was almost as shocking as being shocked. (OK I'm done I'll stop now) God did save me, I was a miracle, I had a purpose and I didn't know how to deal with it. I didn't know if I should tell anyone what had happened to me. I didn't want people to think I was crazy. I didn't want them looking at me like I was one of those "God Freaks" I worked hard to distance myself from church and God, so how was I supposed to talk about Him now? How was I even going to tell my wife and family about what happened?

Plus I felt like a big sinner, why would anyone listen to me about God?

I ended up telling my wife and when she didn't look at me as if I was crazy I told my parents and even a few close friends. I was still rather reluctant to tell my story and I didn't go into a lot of detail. I was really worried about being judged or not believed, plus a part of me didn't feel worthy about talking about God when I was such a sinner, how could I preach about God's love, when God said in the Bible, "If you love me, keep my commandments." Well, apparently I didn't love God because I sure was terrible about keeping His commandments.

The next year was very hard for me. I had quit the fire department a few years previous and was making my living trading the stock market and doing some photography. I was doing really well in the market, I was even teaching stock market seminars across the country. I thought I was on the road to success. There were days I was making over $20,000.

I had the admiration of people both in my life and the people who came to my seminars. I was on top of the world and it all came crashing down all in a year's time. It was springtime and I was married to my wife of fifteen years. We had just gotten sealed in the temple the previous summer. I had just gone through one of the most traumatic things in my life then I died, but at least I still had my marriage and my kids. It could have been worse.

I was making more money than I ever had in my life and everything was great, then the "dot-com" bubble burst and the market crashed. I went from making a ton of money to losing everything I had. Every choice I made was wrong. I was losing hundreds of thousands of dollars a day, and when I did make money it was a fraction of what I was losing.

The "spring 2000 market crash lasted from March 11, 2000, to October 9, 2002. After the bubble burst, online retail companies, such as Pets.com, Webvan and Boo.com, failed completely and shut down along with communication companies, such as WorldCom, NorthPoint Communications and Global Crossing. Others, such as Cisco, whose stock declined by 86%, and Qualcomm, lost a large portion of their market capitalization but survived, and some companies, such as eBay and Amazon.com, declined in value but recovered quickly. [1]

We went on with life and even had our second wedding reception. Things were still good, I had lost money but I had my family, and I was looking for a job. I got one working for another photography studio in Salt Lake City called JayLynn studios. I was doing good, even though I wasn't making the crazy amounts of money that I made before. I was happy. My marriage was better than it had been in years.

---

[1] Wikipedia stock market crash 2000 Dot-Com Bubble

Then the next bubble burst a few weeks after I had my Near Death Experience. I found out my wife was seeing her best friend's husband and they were having an affair. I was crushed. I felt like my guts had been ripped out and replaced with hot coals. I begged her to stay and quit seeing him, but she said she couldn't do that. I felt like everything we had worked for was gone, our money, our temple marriage, everything.

I won't go into a lot of detail about this. I wasn't a victim I was responsible for also creating this. My x-wife is a wonderful person who made some mistakes, just like me. Everything was perfect for both of our learning, but sometimes the learning takes us right to the edge.

We separated as I moved out of my house and into my parents. I was a thirty-four-year-old man back home living with my parents again. I went from rich to broke, married to divorced. I didn't what to do. I ended up getting custody of the kids and moving back into my home after I wouldn't give my ex-wife the house for her and her boyfriend to live in. This was the home I grew up in and bought from my parents. I wasn't going to have him living there with her, so they moved into an apartment, and the kids stayed with me.

Chapter 16
We are all going home.

Lowell Tom Perry (August 5, 1922 – May 30, 2015) was an American businessman and religious leader who was a member of the Quorum of the Twelve Apostles of The Church of Jesus Christ of Latter-day Saints (LDS Church) from 1974 until his death.

I met Elder L. Tom Perry about a year after my divorce and my near-death experience. I had photographed a wedding for a client named Linda. Her daughter, Stacy, had gotten married in the Salt Lake Church of Jesus Christ of Latter-Day Saints Temple.

I was delivering the finished album to Linda at her office which was located at church headquarters in Salt Lake City. Linda was the personal secretary for Elder L. Tom Perry. I remember listening to General Conference where Elder Perry would speak as one of the leaders of the church. He was so charismatic and optimistic. His stories always inspired and uplifted me when I listened to him. Out of all the speakers he was always my favorite.

Elder Perry walked into his office and saw Linda and me at her desk going over the album. He waived and said hello to us and walked to his office door. Elder Perry put his right hand on the doorknob and paused for a few seconds then he turned back to us and pointed at me and said, "You are supposed to come into my office and have a talk with me."

Terror and excitement filled me at the same time. This was one of my childhood heroes, he was considered by church members to be one of the most beloved apostles of the Lord. It was bad enough when I had to go into my bishop and be interviewed and had to confess of my numerous sins to him, but this was a celebrity of the church, a member of the quorum of the twelve apostles.

I nodded my head and walked toward him. I shook his massive hand as it engulfed mine and I followed him into his office. I was filled with apprehension as I said in a chair across from his desk. He started to ask me about my life. What was going on and how I felt about the church.

I told him I had just gotten divorced and I wasn't living my life in accordance with the standards of the church. I had broken my temple covenants and was not living morally clean. He gave me some advice on finding a good girl and getting married as soon as I could.

I then began to tell him about my near-death experience. When I finished telling him about my experience I said, "Elder Perry I don't understand why God didn't pull that lever that dropped the trap door under my feet and I slid down a big slide to be met by a guy in a red suit and carrying a pitchfork."

Elder Perry laughed and said, "Ryan let me ask you one question."

I said, "OK"

He said, "What percentage of anyone who has been baptized by authority unto Jesus Christ will go to the

Celestial Kingdom, (the highest part of heaven where God lives). I looked puzzled and he clarified, "Let's make it simple. What percentage of anyone who is Mormon and has been baptized whether they are active or not will make it to the Celestial Kingdom?"

I thought about it, and all I had been taught about keeping the commandments and enduring until the end. I figured it would not be very many, but I thought I would guess on the high side of what I was thinking. Before you read any more if you are a member of the Church of Jesus Christ of Latter-day Saints I want you to think of a number that feels right to you. This will have some meaning in your life after I tell you what that number means.

I said, "Twenty percent."
He said, "Higher."
I said, "Forty percent."
He said, "Higher."
I said, "Sixty."
He said, "Higher."
I said "Eighty."
He said, "Higher."
I said, "Ninety"
He said, "Higher."
I said "Ninety-five."
He said, "Higher."
I looked at him with a puzzled face and said, "Ninety-six" in an uncertain voice.

He laughed and said, "I think you get the idea. It's going to be a very small percentage that chooses not to."

I said, "I don't understand. I thought we had to be close to perfect, and keep all the commandments and endure to the end."

He said, "What is the requirement to make it into the Celestial Kingdom?"
I said, "Temple marriage?"
He said, "That is the highest degree of the Celestial Kingdom. What is the requirement just to get your foot in the door?
I said, "I am not sure."
He said, "It's baptism."
I felt pretty stupid. If I had known there was going to be a test I might have studied for it. I said, "Oh yeah."

He then asked me what we do when we are baptized. I said, "Ummm we go underwater and they say a prayer over you." I was getting stupider by the minute. I couldn't believe the words coming out of my mouth. This man had to think I was a complete moron.

He said, "We accept the atonement of Jesus Christ in baptism. Before this life in the pre-existence, we accepted Christ's plan and rejected Satan's. We have already accepted the plan twice, do you think in the end when it is offered again we would reject it a third time. The atonement is sufficient to cover any mistakes we will make in this life. The Lord is far more merciful than we think we deserve. There will only be a small percentage who chooses not to accept Christ's gift."

I sat dumbfounded. I had been taught my whole life that you needed to be near perfect and keep all the commandments to be eligible for this reward, and yet here I had a member of the quorum of the twelve telling me something different. Elder Perry understood the atonement. He understood the gift and the mercy of the Lord. I had judged myself to not be worthy of such a gift.

I left Elder Perry with a gift I didn't understand, a gift I would share with hundreds of members of the church if not thousands. It is a gift and a glimpse into the mercy of the Lord. He wants all of His children home, and he has provided a way for every person to receive that gift. We often think like the older brother in the prodigal son, we need to choose right and live perfectly. We think we can earn more than others and we are special. This is not a competition it is a team effort. We want everyone to come home with us. No one left behind.

I prayed about what that percentage meant years later and got the answer that the number you pick represents how you judge yourself. If you pick a low number you are a perfectionist and expect that you should do better than you have, if you pick a higher number you are compassionate with yourself.

I really debated in putting this story in my book and only decided to do so at the last minute while I am finishing this on Maui. I wanted my message to appeal to a large audience, not just Mormons and so I thought of leaving it out. I felt the Lord tell me to put it in and then it was confirmed as I was writing this. My computer crashed three times as I started to write the story. I would get to the same spot in the story and it would crash and none of the versions I had saved along the way would open. I ended up re-writing this part three times before I decided to clear my space from negative entities. After I cleared the space and called on protection from my angels I didn't have any more problems. I have learned when I have a special message to share I get a lot of opposition.

At the time of the message from Elder Perry, I still didn't understand the atonement nor God's mercy. I was still judging myself and feeling unworthy. I went through some tough times over the next few years recovering from the divorce and trying to figure out who I was.

God has created a perfect plan for your life. Just like how each fingerprint is different, and each snowflake is different and unique, your life was designed by God and your highest self to create the perfect path for your learning. This is how much God values you. He spent the time to create a perfect path with perfect teachers to come into your life so you can learn what we need to grow. You are a perfect snowflake crystal and there is a perfect path for you to follow to find your highest self. Imagine the beauty of each unique snowflake and then imagine the beauty of all of the snowflakes combined that make up a blanket of whiteness that covers the earth. God loved you enough to create an individual plan for your growth and happiness. I testify how much He loves you, and how unique and special you are to Him. I pray that you will begin to see yourself as God sees you.

This was a terrible time of adjustment for the kids. My oldest son was fourteen he started drinking and getting into trouble with the law, my second son tried to commit suicide. We had problems upon problems. The next twelve years were a trial, and I was sure I made the wrong choice in coming back to earth. Things started to get a little better in 2004. Business was good and I had my friends from Australia living with me.

They had moved to the U.S. to go to some seminars on self-help taught by T. Harve Ecker. I went to a few of the classes with them and decided to buy a workshop experience called The Enlightened Warrior's Training Camp.

Chapter 17
Warrior Camp

I was single and dated a lot of girls and had a lot of sex outside of marriage. I was a player. I knew I wasn't "doing what was right" or what I had been taught by my religion and my beliefs. I decided I needed some help. Sean Richards my friend from Australia talked me into to going to California with him to this seminar.

I met my second wife at "The Enlightened Warrior Training Camp". This was one of the most amazing experiences of my life. The things I learned and trained in that four-day workshop still effect me to this day. Plus I met my best friend and wife of the next eight years of my life there.

Jessica and I were assigned to be in the same tribe or group. I looked around to find the best-looking women in the group and see if there were any potential women that I might be interested in. My eyes locked with Jessica's. There was an instant recognition. It was like I knew her immediately. From that point on we chose each other as partners when we were asked to pair up. We did all of the activities together. I like to tell people how she tricked me into marrying her.

We were on a group hike exercise. It was really hot. I promised not to divulge the things we did in this workshop so as not to ruin the experience by allowing people's minds to judge and decide about the experience before they do it. But I can say we were on a hike together and it was hot we both just took a drink from our canteens and Jessica pulled out some lip balm. She held it out toward me and asked me if I wanted some? I said sure and reached to take it from her. As my hand moved toward hers she began to pull her's back. I was forced to step forward and again reach for it. As her hand pulled back behind her head and I followed it with my hand and my body, my face came very close to her's and she leaned in and gave me some lip balm that was on her lips. We kissed.

I pulled back in surprise and she giggled, "got ya". I knew right then there was something special about this girl. We helped so many of our tribe up and down the mountain that day. We were the power couple that everyone looked to for help.

I had an experience the next day that I must tell you about and break my promise of silence. It was just too profound of an experience for me not to share it with you. The next day was a spiritual day. We were to do a Native American sweat lodge ceremony. I was a little nervous because I didn't know what to expect.

They split our tribe into two groups; the women were to go into one tent and the men in the other. We had a man in our tribe, Rubin that wore chaos like a cloak, everything he participated in turned into a disaster. He was constantly being injured and causing a lot of drama in the tribe. He required a lot of attention and he didn't care that most of it was negative, as long as we were seeing him he didn't care how he showed up. I think he must have been invisible as a child. I have a lot of compassion for him now and I send him love and encouragement but at the time I was very triggered and annoyed by him.

A sweat lodge or Inipi is described here so you can know what I am talking about.

Inipi - The Rite of Purification

*The Lakota term for sweat lodge is **Inipi** which means 'to live again'. **Inipi** is a purification rite and is necessary in order to help the vision quest seeker enter into a state of humility and to undergo a kind of spiritual rebirth.*

*The sweat lodge is central to **Inipi**. Prayers offered there to draw on all the powers of the universe — Earth, Water, Fire, and Air. In the old days, **Inipi** was done before any major undertaking to purify the body and gain strength and power.*

The actual lodge itself is a dome constructed of 16 young willow trees placed in a circle, traditionally covered with hides so no light could penetrate inside.

On the outside, the formation of the site comprises an earth mound just outside the door of the sweat lodge, facing east, and a fire pit containing stones. The fire represents the sun. Another mound partially encircling the fire pit represents the crescent moon. This is the outer world or cosmos; the inner world is the sweat lodge. It represents the womb of the universe from which souls are created anew.

Prayers are said at each stage of the construction of a sweat lodge. When it is completed, a burning coal is brought in and <u>sweetgrass</u> is burned by the leader of *the **Inipi** to purify the lodge. The pipe is smoked and carried outside, where it is placed on the mound of earth.*

The other participants enter the lodge, sitting in a circle on sacred <u>sage</u>, and the Pipe is brought in and smoked. The heated rocks are placed on the center fireplace and the Pipe returned to the earth mound. Then, the door is closed.

During the ritual, the door is thrown open four times to represent the four ages described by the Sacred White Buffalo Calf Woman. The fourth time, participants leave the lodge, emerging from dark to light which represents the liberation from the physical universe. All that is impure is left in the sweat lodge.[2]

I was a little nervous as I entered the lodge on all fours crawling into the musky darkness. I sure wasn't about to let anyone know my fears. I had been looked at like the wounded superhero that my ego was. I was always the leader who helped everyone. I never asked for help or showed any weakness. I was afraid of letting any weakness show. I had been so terribly weak and sick as a child I loved being looked at with admiration for my manliness. I still struggle with embracing my weakness and faults but I am getting better at loving all of me and asking for help and assistance.

I sat in the inky blackness as the ceremony began. I loved the Native American songs and chants. They were beautiful and called to a part of my soul. I made it through three of the four rounds and we were almost

---

2   http://aktalakota.stjo.org

done with the fourth. I was so drained and exhausted and dizzy from the heat. I had fallen to the earthen floor and breathed the cooler air at the lowest levels of the lodge.

Rubin our master of chaos was screaming about wanting to get out. He was dying, he screamed over and over. Everyone was trying to calm him down, our medicine man, White Buffalo Man was calmly telling him he had to be calm before he exited. He wouldn't calm down and they wouldn't let him exit.

I was so dizzy and fading in and out of consciousness that I got the crazy idea we had to pass out before they would let us out. I started to hyperventilate. I passed out. As everyone exited the tent they tried to get me up and out of the lodge. I have no memory of this time. I guess they got me out of the lodge but as soon as I got out into the light I began to scream.

I remember being in the light and suddenly my body started to transform into stone. It started at my feet and worked its way up my legs. I could see and feel my flesh turning to stone. I screamed in panic. I remember looking at my hand in panic as the last of me turned to stone. I felt trapped in solid stone and I fell over to the ground. My consciousness was aware inside the stone and I worried if this was to be my existence from then on. I would be alive but not be able to talk or to communicate to anyone, as I would be like a statue.

I don't know how long I stayed in this state but it seemed like forever, then I felt a crack in the stone and I could see light shining through the crack. The stone started to crumble and break apart. My hand was made of golden light as well as my arm and as I looked at the rest of my body to my astonishment I was completely made of golden amber colored light. I thought what am I? I had no memory of my life before. I knew I wasn't normally this but I couldn't remember what I had been. I moved my arm through the air in front of me and it made a sound like a lightsaber from Star Wars. I walked around an alien planet with a purple sky amazed and perplexed at what I was.

I lay down on the grass and looked up at the sky. I closed my eyes and when I opened them, the sky turned from purple to blue. I looked around and I saw rolling green hills and blue sky. It looked like a windows screen saver. I was back in my human body. I felt the grass under my hands and felt the breeze on my face. I felt the earth take in a breath. I could actually feel the earth breathe. I started to time my breaths with the earth. I pushed my arms up and I could feel the sky. I felt like I was bench pressing the sky up and helping the earth breathe. It was really crazy.
Then I could see black shadows around me asking me who I was. This in real life was the paramedics asking me if I knew who I was and what was my name. I answered, "I'm nothing", and then I paused and thought no "I'm everything", I amended. I kept repeating that over and over. I am nothing but I am everything.

My best friend that came with me thought I had lost my mind, that something snapped. He told Jessica that I had gone crazy and the paramedics had taken me away. He told her that I could probably end up in a mental institution somewhere and that she should forget about me.

The next thing I remember was a bright light then it pulled back and I saw a man's face. Things started to come into focus. I was looking at a doctor. He asked me if I knew where I was. I looked around and said, "A hospital?"

He told me yes, I had been brought in severely dehydrated and delirious. I joked I am also divorced, all three D's. He looked at me puzzled and continued on like I had said nothing. We are going to keep you on an IV and overnight for observation. Some people had no sense of humor, luckily I had enough for both of us.

I realized I was all alone, no one was there for me and I didn't even have my cell phone. I didn't know anyone's phone number and didn't know who I could call. I slept the night away and in the morning I woke to my phone ringing. I picked it up and said in an inquisitive voice, "Hello?"
"Hi Ryan this is Jessica, do you want to hear from me?"

I said, "YES!! Please, I have heard from no one. Where is Sean Richards I came with?"

"He told me you wouldn't want to hear from me. He's still here at camp. I would like to come to see you. Could I come to the hospital?"

I begged her to come and get me and take me back to camp. I told her I was being released today. She came and got me and we bonded. We were married less than two months later.

I couldn't understand what happened to me or what it meant. I was super tired and stayed a couple more days in a hotel with Jessica and Sean that I rode down with. Sean acted kind of weird toward me and it wasn't too much longer we were no longer friends.

I became severely claustrophobic after this experience. I couldn't even put covers on me all the way, I had to leave one leg out or I would start to panic. It took me a couple of years to get the courage up to do the sweat lodge again. I made it through all four rounds and wasn't claustrophobic anymore.

I got to talk to the medicine man again and asked him what my journey or vision meant. He asked me what it meant to me. I was able to work through the meaning. I had a death in which I was turned to stone. The stone represented no growth, being dead, stagnant, and immovable. I started to crumble and my light shined through. I became light and energy. I then became one with the earth, and then understood the concept of being nothing and everything at the same time. It was way too deep for me to completely grasp at that time, but I could accept it meant something and had a message for me.

Chapter 18
Marriage and Troubles

Jessica and I enjoyed a great friendship and almost seven years of marriage and adventures before our divorce and painful breakup. One day I had an idea for a product. Jessica was a brilliant scientist who had worked for pharmaceutical companies and other research labs. I had the idea for a caffeine-free, sugar-free energy drink. I asked her if she could formulate it.

She said yes she thought she could. We created a product and found a lab to produce it. Once we had a product we needed to raise money to take it to the next level. We had just gotten the money from our insurance claim for her car my son had wrecked.

My son Brandon had just turned sixteen and had his drivers license for only a short time. We had made some t-shirts that said "Vote for Pedro" a line from the movie Napoleon Dynamite. I told Brandon about a festival going on in the town of Preston Idaho where the movie was filmed. I thought he could sell the shirts and make some money. He wanted to go and his little sister Lucy who was eleven was going to go with him. I often have second-guessed my decision to let them go. It now seems reckless and not a good decision.

They were going to take Jessica's Subaru Outback she owned. It was paid for and a good reliable newer car than mine. My youngest son Alex also wanted to go with them up to the festival while they walked around and enjoyed the fair.

We were cleaning out the car to prepare it for them to drive up the ninety minutes it would take them to get there. Brandon and Lucy just got into the car when Jessi yelled to put your seatbelt on. I suddenly remembered I had left a shovel with a broken handle in the back of the car. I went to retrieve that. The head of the shovel had broken off and I was going to return it to the garden store where I bought it. I had a very uneasy feeling until I got the shovel then it wasn't as bad.

I yelled at my youngest son, Alex, who was five. "Hey if you are going with them you better get in the car. They are leaving." Alex turned to Jessi and said, "I'm not going." He seemed really mad about it so she asked him why not. Alex said, "A mean spirit told me I couldn't go."

I walked up to see what the fuss was all about and why Alex went into the house and slammed the door. I met Jessi on the porch and asked her what was up. Just then Brandon honked the car and waved goodbye as they pulled out of the driveway.

Jessi told me what Alex had said to her. I said, "A bad spirit talked to him?" "No" she answered, "A mean one." I went into the house and found Alex in his room face down on his bed and he was crying. I said, "Hey little buddy, what's wrong?" He cried and said a mean spirit told him he couldn't go and he really wanted to.

I asked him what the spirit looked like. He told me he didn't remember. Why did it tell you that you couldn't

110

go? He started crying again and said because it was mean.

This perplexed me but I didn't think he really had a spirit tell him he couldn't go. I figured he was scared and now regretted his decision.

I went to work in my photography studio next door to my house. I had been in there about thirty minutes working on things when my cell phone rang. "Hello?" I answered.

"Hi, you don't know me but I am a truck driver, your kids have been in an accident. I have your son here that wants to talk to you." He handed the phone to Brandon and he came on the line crying and I couldn't understand him.

"Dad I wrecked the car!" He wailed.
"Are you and Lucy all right."? I asked
He cried, "No! Lucy's not breathing!"

My world stopped. My knees buckled. I dropped to the ground. I can not tell you the pain and anguish you feel when you think one of your children may not be breathing because of a car accident. The truck driver took the phone away from Brandon and started talking to me but I didn't hear what he said. I had pulled the phone away from my ear and a moan and cry of despair that feels like the sound is pulling up your guts on the way out escaped my lips.

"Arrrrrrrrrrrrrrghhhhhhhh" I screamed my world going black.

The truck driver kept saying, "Sir! Sir! Sir!" I finally got back on the phone and heard what he said. I took in a deep breath and say a croaky, "Yes"

He said, "Your daughter is fine sir! She's fine! She got knocked out but she's with one of the other truck drivers that stopped to assist. She is talking to him. When we saw your son's car flip and roll three times across the freeway through the median and into oncoming traffic we blocked the road with our semi's. We ran to the accident. Your son was in shock wandering around and your daughter was unconscious in the car, but she came to and is fine. The ambulance just got here and they are taking them to the hospital."

"I asked him again, "Are you positive my daughter is fine? Can I talk to her? "

He took the phone to my daughter and put her on.

"Daddy!" she cried and burst into tears. It took a minute for her to stop crying and talk to me. "Brandon rolled the car when he was playing with the iPod. Dad, I am so scared!"

"Are you hurt? I asked my voice still shaky

"I think I'm ok." She said

I'm coming baby!" I said. "I will meet you at the hospital!"

Both of the kids only had bumps, cuts, and bruises. They were so protected. I think of all the things that led up to the accident. Me taking the shovelhead out of the car, them being reminded to put their seat belts on, Alex getting told he couldn't go by a spirit. If anyone of those things happened differently this story could have ended in tragedy. A box of Kleenex was flying around the car as it rolled and hit Lucy in the head just before her head hit the side window. I can't imagine what a shovelhead could have done!

Chapter 19
Columbia River

In 2009 my wife, Jessica, my youngest son, Alex, and my stepson Chayton went on a road trip. Alex and I had flown up to Alaska to do some fishing, while Jessie and Chayton left to drive to Seattle to visit family. Instead of flying home to Salt Lake we were going to fly to Seattle and drive home with Jessie and do some camping along the Columbia River. We had an amazing trip to Alaska catching salmon, halibut, and rockfish. Alex was eleven years old and was so excited to land a halibut almost bigger than he was. We had gone up there to meet my Dad, my brother, and my brother's son.

It was quite the adventure. I can't tell you how much protection and how hard the angels had to work to keep us alive. We often make the joke about the Rampton guardian angels being the only angels in heaven addicted to coffee and energy drinks just so they can keep up with our shenanigans.

My buddy who lives there is named Ron and he is the kind of guy who likes to fly by the seat of his pants. We borrowed a little 19-foot aluminum boat that looked like an upside down bathtub from one of Ron's friends. We took that little boat off the coast to do some halibut fishing, shrimping, and salmon fishing. We were going to camp that night on the shore but we couldn't find anywhere to tie the boat up. Because of the high and low tides would drop the ocean level so much the water would drop twenty feet in the channel we were fishing. The sun in Alaska doesn't set until 2 am at that time of year. It was just getting dark after a long day of fishing. It was cold, dark, and we were tired by the time we started to look for a place to camp. The shore looked so different at night. We were shinning a powerful spotlight on the land trying to find somewhere to camp. We just couldn't find anywhere that would work. I started to worry that my dad was not doing good.

On the boat, we had Ron and Ron's friend who owned the boat, Craig, Alex and I, my father who was in his eighties, and my brother and one of his sons, Jon. With all of our gear and that many people, the little boat was severely overloaded. If any kind of bad weather came up and the ocean got rough at all we would have sunk. The water was only inches from top of the side of the boat. My dad said he was getting really cold. I wanted to find camp start a fire and get him warmed up, but we couldn't find anywhere that would work to set up camp. There weren't any lights on the boat except for the handheld spotlight that Craig was using to look. So navigating the channel on a pitch black night was hair-raising. I kept worrying that we would hit a log or a big rock that would capsize us.

Finally, we talked Ron into abandoning looking for a campsite and heading back to the marina. It was about fifteen miles away and we had a top speed of between eight and ten knots. We figured it was going to take us about an hour and a half to make it the fifteen miles. Ron opened the engines up to full throttle and we barreled into the blackness, trusting that we wouldn't hit any big rocks or logs as we headed back into Whittier, AK. We had been running at full throttle for about thirty minutes when we ran out of gas. Ron informed us that he had put in the last couple of liters left in the gas can and he prayed we had enough to get us back to the marina. We started up again and followed the GPS course toward warmth, shelter, and food.

We could see the lights of the marina about a mile away when we burned up the last of the gas. The motor sputtered and died. We were so close and yet it seemed so far. No other boats were on the water at three forty-five am. We found the paddles and took turns paddling toward the marina. It took us close to an hour but we finally pulled up to the dock. We decided to just tie up the boat and walk into town and try and find a hotel to stay in so we could get Dad warm and dry.

It was about another thirty minutes walk into town but we found a hotel we could check into and put my dad in the bed with blankets piled up on him. There was a bathtub so we got dad into a warm bath first and then put him into the only bed. The rest of us slept on the floor. We may never know how close we came to death or injury that night, but we could feel the protection and angels helping us that night. We had few other adventures that I'm sure required protection like our halibut fishing trip three miles offshore in four-foot swells on a little boat, but the most dangerous and close call I had on this trip was yet to come.

Alex and I landed in Seattle and Jessica picked us up from the airport. We drove to a campground on the Washington side or the Columbia River. We were going to drive south into Portland tomorrow and on to Boise then home. We stayed in a beautiful campground by the mighty Columbia River. It had a little inlet that created a natural marina and little bay. The water from the Columbia flowed in to make a big circle and flowed back out and to the ocean. The Columbia flows pretty fast and is hundreds of yards wide at

116

the point we are staying. The bay was about two hundred yards across. The water is pretty cold also even though it is mid-August. We had been wading in the water trying to get used to how cold the water was even though the air was one close to one hundred degrees Fahrenheit.

I saw an island in the middle of the bay. I had swum in high school on the varsity team and I thought I was a pretty good swimmer. I started to swim from the shore to the middle of the island. The water was really cold so I was swimming as fast as I could to warm myself up. I would lift my head every few strokes to keep my bearings and see how close I was getting to the island. I was about halfway to my goal when my muscles started to cramp from the cold. My arms curled inward and I couldn't stretch my hands out. I came up for air and looked around. The current from the river had been pulling me away from the center of the bay toward the fast-moving Columbia. I got very concerned I was going to be swept out to the river and then to the ocean. They would never even find my body.

I started to swim back toward shore with all my might, but my arms and legs wouldn't work very well. I started to panic and my vision made the world appear to spin around me in a counter-clockwise motion. My body cramped up I went under and I knew I was drowning. I was fighting to get back to the surface but my body would not cooperate. I was shocked I was drowning. Disbelief and bewilderment flooded my mind. What did I come back from heaven for? It had only been eight years. Had I accomplished anything? Were my kids better off? Did they not need me anymore. All of these thoughts flash through my mind. Then I heard God's voice say to me, "Float on your back. You can float all day."

I relaxed and arched back. I began to float to the surface. My face popped through the water to the sweet air above and I took a breath. Beautiful sweet air rushed into my lungs. I don't think I have ever tasted a breath so sweet. I kept my eyes closed and just relaxed and breathed until I felt my muscles relaxing. My face was the only part of my body out of the water. I don't know how long I was on my back breathing that way, but I hadn't even worried about the current.

I had been in the fast part of the current that was pulling me toward the river. When I finally able to lift my head up and kick my legs to keep me floating I was surprised to find myself almost back to shore where I started. I wasn't even close to the mouth of the bay. I wasn't going to be swept out to sea and drown. I just had to swim about twenty yards to shore.

I was able to swim myself to shore but when I touched the mud at the bottom I didn't have enough strength to pull myself out of the water. Jessica came over and asked if I was okay. I didn't have enough strength to answer I just shook my head. She tried to pull me out of the water but I was too heavy. She yelled for Alex and Chayton and all three were able to pull me up on shore. They got me out of the water and wrapped me up in towels. After about thirty minutes I was able to tell Jessica how close to death I actually was. I told her what happened and the horror on her face turned to gratitude when she realized God saved me again.

Chapter 20
Business Failure

Jessica and I had worked on our business, UpLift Nutrition together for about five years. We had many ups and downs, but we saw our concept go from just an idea to an actual product sold in stores in just a few years. We had put our hearts and souls into this venture. We had some amazing products and good people on our team.

Our company merged with a company that was public. The public company needed a product to make it legitimate and we had the product. We sold our company for stock in the new company. It was what they call a penny stock company. We raised money through the sale of stock. The man who owned the "shell" company was a man named Ed. Ed promised us that he would raise all the money we needed to market the products.

Through greed and dishonest business practices, we were reversed out of the stock and Ed sold our company. We were devastated. We went from being worth millions in stock to less than two thousand dollars. Our income stopped and we ended up losing our house in Farmington. My business partner who is honest and a good man lost his house. We had put everything into our business including our heart and soul. The stress was too much, we started fighting and blaming and all the other things that kill a marriage.

We moved back to our second home in Syracuse and tried to regroup, Jessica got a job in Salt Lake as a scientist and I started my photography business back up. Things got better financially but things kept getting worse in our relationship.

I told Jessica that I was going to move in with my parents and separate from her. She said if I was going to do that she would just move to Salt Lake and get a home closer to her work.

Jessica and I started to drift farther apart. 2012 was the end of the world, well as far as the Mayan Calendar said it would be, but it must have been a prediction about my marriage and not the whole world. Jessica and I filed for divorce. We fought all the time. We both felt it was better to end things now. I thought I would be happier, I thought dating, and having attention from other women would make me feel better about losing our business, but nothing helped me feel whole. I felt shattered.

Chapter 21
Michael

Even after my NDE, I wasn't really religious or spiritual. I was just living life. Then I was told by an angel to paint a portrait of my soul. I didn't understand what that meant. I struggled for a long time deciding if it was my near-death experience I was supposed to write down and teach about. Was I supposed to teach about God's love and how amazing it felt to be in His presence? Was I supposed to write about the amazing things I've been able to do in this life or the many times God saved my life? Was that my message?

Most of the time I felt totally inadequate teaching anything because all I could see was my failures. I would ask myself, "How am I supposed to teach anyone about God when I am a total failure and hypocrite?" I could only see my flaws, not the strength and courage underneath.

Through some life-changing lessons God began to teach me about me, mold me into who He created me to be, who I already was but hadn't "remembered" yet. It is an interesting word. It means to me to join again or be one with the whole again. There are many members of heaven many parts of God. I wanted to become a member of God again. That is where we came from and we will return to. I needed to "Re-Member" now! Become who I had always been not just whom I perceived myself to be for the forty-something years I had been in this physical form.

I had been dating girl named Jade who was quite a bit younger than me. I kept trying to sabotage our relationship and kept running back to my ex-wife Jessica to make sure I wasn't making a mistake. I couldn't make up my mind. Jade was feeling the ups and downs and suggested I go get some energy work done. Jade worked at a salon and spa. There was a lady there who did massage and energy work. I had no idea what energy work was. Jade had bought me a session. I told her I wasn't interested in "woo woo" energy work. That just sounded fake to me. She said I would get a massage. That pushed me over the edge. I decided to go for the session.

I had a session with a lovely lady named Jenny. She just beamed with light from her face. I could feel the spirit of God with her and she was so sweet. I had just stepped into her office when she proclaimed, "OH! You have Michael the Archangel with you!" My brain said, "Who?" Then I noticed my spirit jumping up and down with excitement screaming at the top of its lungs (or whatever spirits use to breathe with) "Oh my God! I love Michael! I love Michael! I love Michael! He is so amazing! He is the most incredible being I know!"

I stopped in my tracks and my brain began to explain to my spirit that we didn't even know who this "Michael" was let alone love him and that it just needed to calm down before someone locked us up for being crazy. My spirit just ignored my brain like the tool it was and just kept going on about its undying love for this being called Michael. My brain began to be more frustrated with my spirit and began swearing at it, but still, my spirit ignored the increasingly frustrated and vulgar brain. Then I heard it.....

A chuckle and then **"I love you too."** Love and warmth flooded my body and my spirit soared, took off and left me with a very shocked and perplexed brain. I felt like a robot from a bad 1960 sci-fi movie where the computer just kept saying, "does not compute!!! Does not compute!!!"

I turned to the lightworker and asked, "Did you hear that?" She asked me what, and I said Michael talked to me and told me he loved me. She beamed and said, "Of course he loves you. You are very dear to him."

I shouted at her, "but I heard a voice! A real voice!" She just smiled and looked at me like a child stating something normal and an everyday occurrence. I shook my head and said well you may think this is normal but this is freaking me out! She just laughed and said we don't have to talk about this, we can just go do your massage.

I almost left right there and then before I even started my session with her, but the girl I was dating talked me into going to see this lady that could help me, "not be such an a-hole".(OK not really her words just my interpretation of them. I decided to stay and get the massage and try and be open to what she was saying.

The massage was great, but the energy work was better. We started to clear some of the blocks I had. She opened up my heart chakra and my crown so I could connect to God.

I believe that this opened me up to what happened over the next few months.

Chapter 22
The Dove

I had invited Jessica to breakfast at my house one morning, I had my youngest son Alex with me and we were making coffee, eggs, and bacon. I was in the middle of making the bacon and outside I heard a car's tire screech on the pavement. It sounded like an accident. The road in front of my house is pretty busy and has a speed limit of 45 mph. I ran out the front door and there was a car stopped in front of my house. There was a man out front looking at something on the road. He walked back and got into his car and drove off.

I wondered if he had hit my cat or the neighbor's dog, so I walked out to the road to check. I saw a beautiful dove that had been hit by the SUV. It was flopping on the road. I approached it and held up a hand to stop traffic. The bird looked like it was dying. It had blood coming out of its eyes and its beak and it had quit flopping about and was lying limp in the road. I picked up the bird and carried it back to my yard.

I prayed to Father in Heaven and asked Him what I should do with the bird. I was thinking that I should put it out of its misery, and I pictured grabbing a shovel and chopping its head off in a quick motion so it wouldn't suffer.

I asked, "Should I put it out of its misery?" I got a firm "NO!" as an answer. Then I heard, "Heal it." I was shocked. Heal it? How was I supposed to do that? I head God repeat, "Heal it!" I shouted back in my mind, " I can't! I don't have the priesthood!" I had been ex-communicated from my church and the priesthood I held or the power to act in God's name with His power was taken away from me. I hear God repeat more forcefully, "Heal it!"

I had argued with God enough I decided to give it a try but I didn't know the right way to do it. I shut my eyes and just imagined God's light coming from heaven and entering the top of my head traveling down through my arms to the bird. I felt something happening, like electricity or warmth coursing through me. I felt a peace and calmness come over me; and a feeling like being wrapped in a warm blanket.

Was it working? Was I healing the bird? I felt the warmth and electricity stop and I opened my eyes. I imagined the bird would be healed and fly out of my hands it was so powerful what I felt. The bird still lay in my hands faintly twitching. I was so disappointed. Was I having delusions of grandeur? Was I fooling myself that God spoke to me? Was I going crazy or thinking I was more than what I was? I wasn't anything special, and I didn't even have a religion anymore. Even the church thought I was a loser. I walked over by my front porch and put the dead bird under a bush and went into the house to check on the bacon I had turned to low on the stove.

I was just putting the bacon onto some paper towels to soak up the grease when God said go check on the bird. I was like oh no, maybe my cat was eating it! I ran out the front door and looked for the bird but it wasn't where I left it. I looked around for feathers and I saw it had moved a few feet and was standing up on its feet looking around as if it was stunned. It shook it's feathers like it was shaking off water. I yelled into the house, "Jessica! Alex! Come out and see what has happened. They came running out the door just as the bird flew into the air and over to the big pine trees next door.

I said, "Did you see that!? That was amazing! That was the dead bird! Jessica looked puzzled, and said, "Maybe it was just stunned." I just shook my head and marveled at God's miracle and I got to be a part of witnessing it.

The next day I had gone to work. I sat at my desk pondering what had happened. I was amazed at what God had done. I felt a little chagrinned because this happened on a Sunday morning and the previous Friday I had lost my wallet and I was so mad at God. I remember yelling at him that I was writing my book and bad things were still happening to me. I was so mad. I was really ashamed of how I acted with God over losing a stupid wallet when He just showed me a miracle.

I cried and thanked Him for the miracle and begged for forgiveness about losing faith. I got done with my prayer and started working on my computer again. I got up to go to the bathroom when I noticed my wallet sitting right there by the monitor! Had it been there the whole weekend and I threw a fit over nothing? Yet God still showed me a miracle? Or had an angel found it for me and put it there? I didn't know, but I left work feeling completely grateful for what happened and how merciful God was.

I remember feeling in awe of God and I pulled into my driveway. I got out of my car and the two doves who lived next door in the big pine tree flew over and landed on my fence less than six feet away from where I was standing. I was pretty sure one of them was the one that God had healed. I stood there transfixed to my spot and the three of us just looked at each other. The doves turned to each other made some dove sounds and then looked back at me. We stared at each other for about another five seconds and then they flew away.

Today there is a whole family of doves living in the tree. I see eight of them flying around my house. I have never gotten within fifty feet of them since before they fly away, so I am pretty sure that was a miracle too.

I am really surprised at myself right now while I am writing this and reading what I am writing. God has shown me time after time that He has my back and I just need to trust Him, but I look back and even though the lesson was clear with the doves, I still would get upset with God and demand He does something now over and over the past five years. I hope that I have finally learned my lesson and will trust God with all my heart, I will be patient, and I will wait for my prayers to be answered in His time.

Chapter 23
My God change Part 1

January 1st, 2013.
Even after all of the spiritual things that happened to me, (just hearing an angel's voice), and feeling more connected and spiritual than I had in years, I really wasn't very big on talking about God, I wasn't even praying that much, let alone having any spiritual foundation. I was still worried about being judged, and I viewed myself as a sinner. Why would people listen to a sinner talk about God? Someone righteous man should be doing that not a sinner like me.

I had so many regrets about my marriage. I had lost my best friend, I wasn't happy dating. I just wanted my old life back. I tried to start dating Jessica again. She wasn't sure if I would break her heart again so it was difficult to get her to agree to take me back let alone go on a few dates. I asked her if I could take her to the hot springs for her birthday at the end of December. She agreed and we drove up to Idaho.

The trip was my last ditch effort to save my failed marriage. I didn't tell Jade I was taking my wife to try and reconcile. Jessica and I had been separated for about nine months, and I was still in love with her but she wasn't ready to forgive me and I didn't want to lose what I had with Jade.

I didn't like myself at the time. In fact, I hated myself. I was hoping that if enough people loved me, maybe I would feel love. So that summer I had gone from relationship to relationship. I really liked Jade but I was afraid I was getting too close and it would just end in disaster, like my marriage. We had lost the casualness of the relationship and it was getting too serious, so I decided if I was going to be in a real relationship why not try to salvage my marriage? I don't think I have ever been more confused or indecisive in my life. OK people who know me are rolling their eyes right now…. (Ryan you are always this way! This is your pattern.) UGH shhhh, don't confuse me with the facts people. Let me tell my story in a romantic way.

Ok to this day, I still have some of the same pattern running. The difference is I can say I love myself more and I am learning to love and forgive myself on a daily basis. They say our mess is our message. Well, I have a big mess. I should come with one of those warning labels. Caution he's a fallible human. Proceed with caution.

I really felt my life was a terrible mess. I had failed in my second marriage, lost a business that was potentially worth millions, had my dreams crushed, and bounced from woman to woman trying to feel loved. I used to lay alone in bed at night and punch myself in the head and cry myself to sleep saying what an idiot I was.

I also felt so much pressure from being a Mormon and not being perfect. I felt like God must be so disappointed with me. I loved God and believed in Christ but no matter how hard I tried I always failed. I knew I just needed to love God more than my sins and try a little harder, but I always failed. Always gave in to my carnal appetites. I was evil, I was wicked, I was a piece of crap, and I deserved to die and go get my punishment of eternal failure of being stuck in a place where God wasn't because I didn't deserve to be in His presence.

I obviously didn't love God. I was told over and over "If you Love Me keep My commandments." I thought I loved God but obviously, other people loved Him more. Every time I got up and tried to be a good Mormon I fell down into my sins and my personal hell again. I began to think I should not even try any more all I do is fail.

I was so miserable with myself that I often thought of suicide. I used to sit in the shower with the water off and put my forty-caliber Smith and Wesson handgun in my mouth. I wanted desperately for the pain to be over. I sat in the shower because I didn't want to leave a mess that others had to clean up. I was a firefighter and an EMT on the ambulance for years. I knew what kind of mess a gunshot to the head would leave. I didn't want to leave a mess.

As bad as the pain was, I kept thinking of my kids, and how devastated they would be if I pulled the trigger. It stopped me every time. Thank God I didn't ever take that way out and ended my own life prematurely. This life is our laboratory to learn in the physical realm. If we end it before our time I believe there are consequences in the afterlife. We do not go to the peace that I felt when I electrocuted myself on accident. I believe we feel intense sorrow compounded by the all those that loved us and now were grieving for our loss. I believe we feel all of their pain and ours. The spirits I have talked to that have passed by suicide are fighting such a battle to overcome their mistake. They have told me we can accomplish more in five minutes in this life in growth and learning than they can in a thousand years. It is intensely more difficult to learn what we could have on earth when we take our own life and give up.

Anyone who feels the need to end their life, please listen to my words of encouragement. Do not give up. You are loved. Please call upon God as I did, forgive yourself for everything, understand that you are perfect and the pain is only temporary. Tomorrow is a new day and everything can change for the better. Sometimes God takes us to the edge, that is where the most learning can occur, but He always provides a way out, if we just trust Him.

Please understand you are not alone, you are not the only person to feel the way you do. I must have thought or tried suicide at least a two dozen times, but I found a way to make it one more day. You can too, one step at a time. I am so thankful for my life now. Life is a gift. Our opposition and challenges are a gift. If you could see the other side as I have you would see what a precious gift each hard thing we go through is. Going through challenging times is something we were excited for before we came to this earth life, it's hard but something that when we look back on life we will be filled with immeasurable joy for the lesson. While we are in the middle of the challenge it's pretty hard to have that outlook. It's ok to bitch, moan, and complain, just don't give up. It's easier if you have a positive outlook and understand everything is for your learning and growth and have the faith that God will help you through it.

Just remember you are loved beyond words beyond comprehension. You are precious, unique and beautiful. I love you and my spirit is here to serve you. My highest self-recognizes your highest self.

You can not change your past... Or can you? Sometimes our past is very painful and hard to remember and relive. Some of our memories are so painful and we want desperately to change what happened. The past is the past it doesn't have to dictate our future, but it does.

Our patterns run in our sub-conscious dictating how we feel and choose. We often stay stuck in the same patterns of not being enough, not being worthy, or being unlovable. We let our past memories settle in our sub-conscious and create our future.

If we choose to change our past through the atonement of Jesus Christ and allow forgiveness and love to transmute those memories back to love we can change our future by changing our past. Everything is a story that we have made up in our head to describe what happened to us in the physical realm. The story isn't exactly true, it's just how we interpreted what happened to us. If we choose to send love and forgiveness to that memory and allow the pure love of God to transmute that memory we can change our pattern, and change our future.

Chapter 24
Ho'oponopono

Using Ho'oponopono the Hawaiian rite of forgiveness we can change the past through love.

I'm sorry
Please Forgive me
I love you
Thank you

Directing Ho'oponopono toward those memories that are creating the feelings that are keeping you stuck is the key to unlocking your *future*. If you want better relationships, more money, more happiness pay attention and use this magic to change your life.

Find the feeling that is your emotional black hole and that is defining your actions and keeping you stuck, send massive love and forgiveness to that memory. Repeat the words over and over in your head or out loud whatever feels the best to you. This make take some time or it could be immediate, it all depends on how long it takes for your subconscious to let go. I talk more about this toward the end of the book.

You can not change your past... Or can you? Sometimes our past is very painful and hard to remember and relive. Some of our memories are so painful and we want desperately to change what happened. The past is the past it doesn't have to dictate our future, but it does.

Our patterns run in our sub-conscious dictating how we feel and choose. We often stay stuck in the same patterns of not being enough, not being worthy, or being unlovable. We let our past memories settle in our sub-conscious and create our future.

If we choose to change our past through the atonement of Jesus Christ and allow forgiveness and love to transmute those memories back to love we can change our future by changing our past. Everything is a story that we have made up in our head to describe what happened to us in the physical realm. The story isn't exactly true, it's just how we interpreted what happened to us. If we choose to send love and forgiveness to that memory and allow the pure love of God to transmute that memory we can change our pattern, and change our future.

Each part of the words of Ho'oponopono utilizes the Godhead.

I'm sorry brings you in humility. You are no longer angry or hurt, you no longer let this experience define who you are. You are sorry for letting this control you or you are sorry for your actions, either way, you are coming to the altar in humility. Your "ego" and "pain-body" are checked at the door only humility accompanies you forward to this sacred rite.

Please forgive me calls upon the atonement of Jesus Christ. It uses the power of his ultimate sacrifice to clean and erase the energy surrounding the event and memory that is keeping you stuck. Using the ultimate power of forgiveness can transmute any negative energy stuck in your subconscious that is keeping you in a pattern.

I love you calls upon the power of God and His unconditional love. Unconditional love is what you are made of and what your soul desperately wants to remember. It heals all, physically and spiritually. It fills every hole and emptiness in your soul and completes you. It can change all from addiction to self-loathing, from physical ailments to a broken spirit. It brings us home.

Thank You calls upon the Holy Spirit in the form of gratitude. The universe and God gives you more of what you focus on and when you are focused on gratitude you will receive more of what you are grateful for. This completes the process and the rite of clearing and forgiveness.

Chapter 25
God Change Part 2

So back to Lava Hot Springs and my **God Change**.
I was broken in every sense of the word, mentally,
physically, and spiritually. I was done. Past done. I
wanted to go home. I wanted to be done with this life.

Jessica and I were in different parts of the pool. I was
alone about twenty or thirty feet away from anyone else
in the big hot springs pool. I decided to pray.

My prayer was not just a prayer, it was a plea, I plead
for God to take me home. I cried, "I made a mistake God,
I should not have chosen to come back to my kids, I
should have stayed with You. I am more wicked now
than when I died. I know I have blown any chance I had
to be with You again." My soul ached for heaven. I
wanted to go home and I begged God to take me. I
understood on some level I could never commit suicide,
but I hoped He would drop a meteor out of the sky on
top of me or hit me with lighting. My sins over the last
year were so much worse than before when I died. I was
sure that I had blown any chance I had to go to heaven.

Thoughts of other people's councils on my near death
experience also rang in my head. I had one devout
Mormon lady tell me that when God asked me if I
wanted to come home with Him, He really wasn't taking
me to heaven. He was taking me to spirit prison to pay
for my sins.

I thought, "What if she was right? What if even then I wasn't worthy of going home to live with God?"

That thought makes me chuckle now. God's love isn't conditional. He doesn't love us more if we are righteous or less if we are sinners. It's all-encompassing.

I felt horrible and wanted to die, I so wanted this life to be over and I could just go home. I'd be happy to be the lowest of servants for God, just put me in a corner somewhere and I get to clean up elephant poop.

God spoke to me the first time since twelve years previous when He asked me if I had asked for help. He spoke in a voice that was powerful yet quiet, came from everywhere but was in my ears and in my heart. I was profoundly changed by what He said to me; ***"Leaving my presence one time is traumatic for everyone on the planet because you leave nothing but love. For you to remember what My love felt like, and chose to leave a second time has left such a hole in you that you have tried to fill it with everything but Me, but what you really want is Me."***

I felt something clunk in place. It was a physical clunk, like an internal switch being thrown on or a piece of the puzzle finding it's home. I was exuberant! I shouted at the top of my lungs, "Dude!!!! I'm yours!!!!!"

I knew I was God's and He was mine. I felt so connected to Him. I no longer felt like a human being that had a spiritual experience. I felt like an eternal spiritual being having a physical experience. This was the most defining moment of my life. I promised God that I would devote my life to Him. I would talk about Him and His love every day. I would not be ashamed. I would not shrink from shouting His name from the rooftops. I would no longer live to make money or get rich or get the applause of others. I dedicate everything I am and everything I own to God. I am His servant, His messenger.

I walked around for the next two weeks in a bliss cloud. It was the most amazing time of my life. I was so happy, so fulfilled, so complete. I had amazing spiritual experiences, some of which I will share and some which are personal and sacred to me that won't be in this book. It was two weeks of education instruction from God and how perfect His love is.

Chapter 26
Homeless Woman

One of the most amazing experiences I had during this time was when I was walking down the street and a homeless woman approached me begging for money. She was probably in her thirties but looked seventy. She had meth sores all over her face, rotten brown teeth, and wild unkempt hair. I told her I didn't have any money and started to walk away from her. In my mind, I judged her harshly. I called her repulsive and thought what terrible choices she had made to get herself in that situation.

Immediately I heard God, He asked, "Would you like to see how I still see my daughter?" I stopped in my tracks, said yes and slowly turned back toward the woman. An image like a hologram appeared floating in front of her face I could still see her through it but the image that floated was that of an angel. She was beautiful with bright eyes, white teeth, gorgeous hair and a beautiful smile and countenance that showed her inner beauty. I was dumbfounded. I stared at her and couldn't speak with my mouth agape and trying to form words.

She looked at me like I was the village idiot who's cheese slid off his cracker. I finally found my words, and asked her, "Do you know how God sees you?" She replied, "Huh?? I'm not religious!" I asked her if she believed in God? She replied she did. I asked her when was the last time she had prayed to Father? She replied it was a long time ago. I told her of what had just happened to me and how God saw her. She began to cry.

I gave her a hug and felt her amazing spirit. I walked away from her vowing to get better at not judging God's children. I wanted to see people the way God saw them, beautiful and without sin.

Chapter 27
Losing the Spirit.

About the third week after my change, I felt the spirit began to slip from me, where I felt God's presence less and less each day. I desperately tried to find the cause. Was I being wicked? Did I have bad thoughts what was changing? What was driving the spirit away? I prayed to God, "What am I doing wrong? What have I done to offend thee? How can I get your spirit back? The answer I got back was both profound and thought-provoking. God said, "I have carried you for the last few weeks, I have set you down and am walking beside you, you need to learn to connect to me."

I was relieved and perplexed. I was happy it wasn't due to my actions, but what did I need to learn to connect to God? How could I be with Him every day? How could I keep Him in my heart? I tried becoming a super Mormon. I went back to church after a seven-year absence; I started keeping the word of wisdom (quit drinking coffee, beer, and wine) and went and confessed my sins to my bishop.

Chapter 28
Old Coin

I was excited to be back at church, learning and serving God. I was trying my best to change all my wicked ways and give myself completely to God by proving I was worthy and I was righteous. I went this way for a couple of months and then one night I messed it all up. I wasn't dating anyone. I had broken up with Jade and Jessica and I was just working on being the best me I could be. I felt like I needed to be abstinent and for me to be that I couldn't date anyone.

A woman on Facebook hit me up and asked me out. She was young and beautiful. I went over to her house to meet her in person to take her to dinner. When I got there she asked if it was ok we stayed there and watched a movie. Halfway through the movie we started making out, one thing led to another and we had sex. I left her house devastated. I was so upset with myself for failing God. How dare I give myself to God and dedicate my life to him and the first lovely girl that bats her pretty eyes at me I commit one of the "worst" sins. I couldn't have felt lower about myself. I went home and prayed for hours on my knees. Crying to the Lord. Begging for His forgiveness. I picked out the biggest mental stick I could find and began to beat myself up with it. I told myself what a piece of poo I was for failing the Lord. I hated my dark side. I wanted to purge it, wash it clean, purify myself so that God would know that I loved and followed Him.

I prayed that way for over an hour until my knees ached and my eyes were puffy from crying. I finally got into bed. Just after I shut out the light and started to relax I saw something weird appear before my eyes. I was wide-awake but I thought I must be dreaming, hallucinating or having a stroke, this couldn't be real. I saw a gold coin about the size of a salad plate floating about a foot in front of my face. It looked like an old Roman coin with a man's face on it. I rubbed my eyes and waved my hand through the coin but it didn't waiver or change. It just floated there. I've never seen anything like it before or since. I was trying to figure out what I was seeing when I heard God's voice simply say, ***"This is you."***

This is me? What does that mean? There was a pause and then the coin started to turn. It spun all the way around to the tail side of the coin. The other side of the coin was dirty and corroded not near as shiny and pure as the front. Then God said, ***"I love both sides of you."***

I didn't really understand this concept until a few years later. I thought I understood it, but I finally grasped the fullness of this statement when a few more of the pieces of the puzzle fell into place.

God just doesn't love the good or righteous side of you, He also loves the side of you that sins, that makes mistakes, the dirty side, the shadow side. He loves all the parts that make us who we are. He loved the homeless woman and did not judge her the way that I did. He loved the whole coin, the beautiful angel her spirit was and the disaster her physical form was. The

144

coin did not lose value just because one side of it was dirty. If you dropped a gold coin into the mud and one side was covered in filth would the coin have less value? No the gold's value remains the same it just needs a little washing to make it pure again. That is what the atonement does. It washes our coin clean and restores the value we think we have lost because of the dirt we have picked up on our journey.

God loves both sides of you. He loves the perfect spirit that is experiencing life as who you are and He loves the physical being with all its flaws and imperfections. "All your curves and all your edges, all your perfect imperfections", to quote a beautiful song by John Legend.

Chapter 29
Jesus Christ Vision

I went to sleep puzzling what had happened to me. What did the coin mean? could God love the bad side? Does He love the bad side but still want us to scrub it clean? I was so confused with what I had been taught in the scriptures and in church and what God was teaching me now.

I finally fell asleep and had the most vivid dream. I dreamt I was in a forest of scrub oak and trees. The vegetation was thick. I was carrying a large canvas sack on my back. I had an urgency to get out of the forest. I was rushing and pushing my way through the thick branches. They were scratching my face, and catching on the bag and my clothing. It seemed every step I was hindered and pulled back and I tried to get out of the woods. I felt someone walk up beside me. I could only see their legs from the knees down due to the dense bushes. The man was wearing a white robe and was wearing leather sandals. I recognized my Savior immediately.

I dropped to my knees and began to cry. "Give me your burden," Jesus stated. I grabbed the sack tightly and hugged it. "No." I sobbed "This would hurt you. I love you too much. I can't give it to you."

He said, "Give me your burden." Again I hugged it tighter and cried. A third time he asked, "Give me your burden as I have already paid for it. It is mine to bear now." The words pierced my soul. Of course, He had.

Why was I being so stubborn? I pushed the sack toward Him. He knelt before me and took my face in His hands. He had the most beautiful blue-green eyes, plus many other colors in complex forms that I cannot describe. Jesus looked at me with those piercing eyes and said, "Your sins are forgiven you" He said. I began to cry with Joy and relief. I woke up in my bed crying. I saw a painting a few years after by a young lady named Akiane Kramarik from Illinois that looked a lot like who I saw the eyes were the same but His hair was different.

I felt clean, forgiven. I had begun to understand how God saw me. He didn't see me as I saw me. I saw me as broken, un-fixable, a failure, destined to screw up time after time. God saw me as my perfect soul, the warrior angel who serves and loves His children. He saw my dark side as lessons for my highest good. I saw my dark side as the "real" me. I thought I was my mistakes, I identified with my lessons instead of the highest self, my soul that watched and learned from my mistakes.

Chapter 30
God's Love and Mercy

God just doesn't love us when we are righteous, He made us, programmed our personality to teach us the most about us, what we wanted to learn. We came with our bags packed as far as personality, faults, and temperament go. I believe God designed us with what was best for our highest learning and highest path. The lessons, mistakes, and opposition we experience are all for our betterment, learning, and growth.

Trying to willfully overcome sin through our efforts is like taking a bath. Spirituality is represented by water. As we climb into the tub and immerse our self into accepting God and Christ into our life our sins float to the surface and we become aware of them much like a bunch of ping pong balls poured into your bathwater. The balls float on the surface. We try our best to hold them down. When we focus on one ball we can hold it underwater, but all the others stay floating and since our focus is on the one ball we become unaware of all the other "sins" that are floating on the surface. We have mastered holding the one sin at bay, immersing the ball hiding it.

We might even become good at holding quite a few balls underwater and taking pride in the fact that we have very few sins floating for others to see. We judge our self on our ability and our worth based on this ability on overcoming sin and judge our self to be a good an righteous person.

Or we may look at all the balls floating and feel overwhelmed in the fact that we are beset with so many sins, so many balls floating. We give up on even trying to hold them underwater. We may even get out of the bath and vow to not get in the tub again. Many give up on God when they realize they have more ping pong balls floating than others. Sometimes we throw God out with the bathwater and decide because of our religion and the things we were taught doesn't work for us so we not only reject the teaching that does not work, we reject it all. We reject God, that pure source of love and peace.

Imagine that Christ and the atonement is one giant vacuum. As soon as you turn over the effort of holding the balls underwater and give the task to the Savior, it is done. He turns on the big vacuum and magically the balls float up out the water and sucked into the tube. There is no more frantically holding them down.

Some people take pride in the fact that they were born with less ping pong balls than others. They feel superior. They want to point out to others that they have a lot of balls floating on the surface of the water, and that they need their brand of religion or do what they are doing. They believe their path is the only way to get rid of the sins. They proclaim they have no balls floating. I have submerged my ping pong balls in the water. I am so holy. They are not holy the sins are still there. Only Christ can remove them from the whole of the water, not just the surface.

There have always been people who try and make it harder than it is meant to be. They want to show their love and devotion to God by going the extra mile. They add to the requirements, restrictions, conditions, and rituals to the equation of the atonement.

In the middle ages, certain monks practiced corporal mortification of the flesh. In simple terms, this can mean merely denying oneself certain pleasures, such as permanently or temporarily abstaining (i.e. fasting), from food, alcoholic beverages, sexual relations, or an area of life that makes the person's spiritual life more difficult or burdensome. Some took the extreme even further to self- flagellation. They would beat their backs and body with whips, rods, and other instruments to cause pain and suffering. In their mind, this would help them focus their devotion to God and show others their pious nature how dedicated they were to their religion and their love of God.

One nun, Sister Johnson, who served with Mother Theresa was interviewed and talked about her first session of self-flagellation. *"My knees shook. I took the bunch of knotted cords into my hands. From Sister Jeanne's stall, I heard the beating sounds, one, two, three. . . . I swung harder. The skin of my lower thighs turned red, then red with white streaks as I hit harder."*

When I took that rope whip into my hands, I was scared, I was excited, I hoped that I was on my way to conquering my selfishness and becoming a holy person. When you visit the homes and shrines of various saints, you often see hair shirts or whips or spiked chains on display. This is a religion in which nearly every house of worship, classroom, and private home has as its most prominent feature the image of a bloodied, tortured man. We were taught that wearing spiked chains and beating ourselves allowed us to share in his work of redemption.

In the Jewish religion, faithful Jews had many restrictions, such as how many steps you could take on the Sabbath. What clothing you could wear, what food was holy to eat and what was not and would be a sin.

Religion of all sorts uses these techniques to become holier, a purified sacred vessel without sin or blemish. They believe is God requires this then I will take it a bit farther just to prove my love for God is superior to everyone else. It becomes a competition and a way to gauge one's place in God's heart. He must love those who sacrifice and keep His laws and rules even more than He loves anyone else. Or is His love "unconditional"?

I was taught by my religious leaders that I needed to be punished for my sins, that I needed to prove to God I would follow His word. It was all up to me. I can now see the pattern. I felt bad about my sinful nature, I would self-punish, verbally abuse wear mental sackcloth and ashes, and find reasons to hate that part of me that wanted to sin. I thought I could beat it out of me.

I felt like the mental pain of my sins was so great that physical pain must be better. I know people who cut themselves, put hot cigarettes on their skin, slept on the floor, and other ways to cause pain. I seemed to favor putting myself down inside my head. I felt like a complete failure. I was destined for great things but I was a loser, an utter failure, a colossal disappointment to God and myself.

So you can see why I was so shocked and uncomprehending on why God would love both sides of me. How could that be? Didn't God hate sin? Didn't he hate the wicked and poured out His wrath upon them?

If anyone was deserving of wrath it was me. So why did God love both sides of me? How can he love the part that is sinful, the part that enjoys sin?

Let's see how Paul describes it in Colossians; This is where Paul is preaching to the church in Laodicea. These are the people who have accepted Jesus Christ and His teachings.

Paul wants us to be encouraged and knit together by strong ties of love. He wants us to have complete confidence that they understand God's mysterious plan, which is Christ Himself.[3]

God's plan is a plan of love, a plan of peace, a plan of forgiveness and mercy. In Christ lie hidden all the treasures of wisdom and knowledge. [4]

---

[3]   NLT Colossians 2:2
[4]   NLT Colossians 2:3

Paul says this so no one will deceive you through well-crafted arguments. And now that you have accepted Jesus Christ as your Lord, you must continue to follow him.

He councils to let your roots grow down into Him, and let your lives be built on Him. Then your faith will grow strong in the truth you were taught, and you will overflow with thankfulness.[5]

You were dead because of your sins and because of your sinful nature. Then God made you alive with Christ, for he forgave all our sins.

God wants our hearts to dwell upon Him. He doesn't want us to make up extra rules that make us proud of our righteousness.

You have died with Christ, and He has set your free from the spiritual powers of this world. So why do you keep on following the rules of the world, such as, "Touch not, taste not, handle not." Such rules may seem wise because they require strong devotion, pious self-denial, and severe bodily discipline. But they provide no help in conquering a person's evil desires.[6]

Don't drink this, don't use that, these are all evil things. If you abstain from them you will be special, more righteous, pious, set apart from the world. Is this true? Is that what God wants? I believe He wants us to be

---

[5]   NLT Colossians 2:7
[6]   NLT Colossians 2: 20-23

happy, enjoy life, focus on Him, on love, on forgiveness, on charity, and on loving your neighbor not judging your neighbor.

Let God and Christ be the vacuum that lifts your sins up, let yourself not judge others and say that they need to repent. Be the love, be the good that you already are. Love one another. Be kind and embrace your highest path. Embrace what you are and learn from what you are not. Condom not your flaws, but love them, and send them forgiveness.

"Peace be still and know that I am." We worry too much. We worry about our salvation, we worry about our children. God has told me time after time when I come to Him with my worries and concerns, "Peace be still." How many times have I questioned God and worried if I was on the right path if I was even supposed to write this book? How many times did I get mad at God because I didn't get the answer I wanted immediately? How many times did I lose faith, question my own beliefs, or let fear control me? Every time the answer was peace be still.

Chapter 31
Motorcycle Accident

On March 26th, 2016, at about nine in the morning, I was riding my motorcycle up to meet my kids for breakfast. Normally my girlfriend would have been on the back of the bike with me but we had gotten into a fight the day before and we were not talking.

I love riding my motorcycle. I love the raw power, the speed, and the freedom you feel. I rarely wore a helmet. My family and especially my mom would chastise me for not, but I would just argue, "I can't die. The Lord will protect me, I've even tried to commit suicide and the Lord wouldn't let me, nothing bad is ever going to happen." (Famous last words.)

Remember the part I said about being humble? Yeah, apparently I needed another lesson on why we should be humble, and not cocky or arrogant. I was riding north on main street and I was almost to the café where I was meeting my kids. I had just turned the corner and accelerated up to about fifty miles per hour. I saw a brown car pull out of McDonald's and stop with her left turn signal on. I was approaching her and so I made sure I made eye contact with her. It was a young girl driving probably about sixteen or seventeen.

I saw her look at me and so I looked back at the road in front of me. That is when she pulled out and turned left in front of me. I grabbed the hand brake and stepped on the brake pedal simultaneously. Her car was right in front of me about 30 yards away I knew I was going to hit her side of the car. I instinctively laid the bike down so the bike would skid and the tires would hit and provide some buffer between my body and the car.

My left foot caught the asphalt and I flipped off the bike and cartwheeled down the road. I hit my forehead off center toward my left temple and I flipped into the air I hit my boots then my knees and my head was fast approaching the asphalt again. I pulled my chin down as the back of my head hit the road. I didn't feel like hard asphalt it felt soft like hands were holding my the back of my head and cushioning the blow.

I flipped again and hit my knee again then my left shoulder and I skidded down the road and came to a rest in front of an approaching car. I had the wind knocked out of me and my bell was rung pretty hard. My ears were ringing and I could feel blood trickling down my face. I just laid there trying to figure out how bad I was hurt. People came running up to me asking if I was ok? I nodded my head yes. It was then I could feel my phone going off in my pocket. I answered the call it was my oldest son. He asked me where I was, and I said laying in the middle of the road. He said, "Was that you? I drove right past that and said look at the poor guy!" I said I couldn't talk right then.

Sean, my oldest, ran across the street and up to me worried out of his mind. "Dad are you OK?" I said I think I am and then the ambulance showed up and took me to the hospital. I ended up with a traumatic brain injury that affected my speech for about six months. I have some gaps in my memories and every once in a while I still stutter, but I was lucky and blessed to be alive. I didn't realize how many things slightly different would have ended in my death. If I hadn't laid the bike down, if Michael the Archangel hadn't put his hands on my head and cushioned the blow to the back of my head, I would have died on the street.

A few days later another motorcycle was hit at the intersection and the rider died in a very similar accident. I know I was protected again and kept from being seriously injured even though I chose to learn a hard lesson through my arrogance. I needed constant reminders to stay humble.

I learned to not tempt God, just because I was protected and being kept here to finish my mission didn't mean that I couldn't be hurt or even hurt badly. I look at life as a gift and I am grateful that the Lord has been so patient and loving toward my stupid human self. I know who I am, I am a warrior for God and I have a purpose and a mission that I am here to fulfill. I know you do too. I want to bring out that warrior in you. It's my prayer that my words touch a part of your soul that knows of your spiritual gifts and of your purpose to realize your highest self.

Chapter 32
You were born a warrior.

This is more than a statement or a cliché, this is truly your purpose in being here. You came to this earth to fight the battle of duality. You are both good and bad, both light and darkness, both sickness and health.

The warrior fights not for the country, nor to kill the enemy. A warrior fights for love. He or she fights for the brother or sister next to them. They fight to save the ones they love. A warrior fights to know thyself. A warrior fights to keep their commitments.

What image do you have of a warrior? Do you imagine knights in shining armor, or a samurai holding his sword above his head bellowing his war cry? What does it mean to be a warrior for Christ, or for God, or for the light? How do you see yourself? Can you see the warrior in you? We all fight the battle of duality. We are all light and dark, both an angel and a demon. We have a soul that is light and love and at times feel like we are darkness and shadow. The battle we fight is to return to the light, remember who we are, allow ourselves to shine our highest self.

I want to teach you to fight to know yourself, your whole soul. I want you to return to love and self-love and forgiveness, but you have to be brave, you have to be committed. You would fight and die to save someone you love but will you fight the hardest fight you will ever have, the fight to forgive yourself to change your limiting beliefs and return to the love that you are? I love thinking that we are warriors repairing creation. We are constantly repairing memory and mistakes. We repair with love. We can help repair someone's life with a few kind words or even a smile.

I want you to fight for love. Love one another, love yourself and love God. Fight to share love, spread love and forgiveness, let's repair the damage that this life does. Let's save a few people from this life of contrasts and duality, where we are constantly being damaged.

In quantum physics "Schrodinger's Cat" is a theory that all subatomic particles exist in two states until observed. Schrodinger explained; *Imagine there is a cat in a box, it is both alive and dead simultaneously until the moment it is observed and chooses a form.* Subatomic particles have been proven to share this behavior. Quarks exist in two forms until observed then one manifests.

So why would you be an exception in the laws of the universe? You are not. You exist in two forms on multiple levels. You exist both as a physical being and a spiritual one. You exist as both masculine and feminine. You contain both the "male" hormone testosterone and the female opposite estrogen. You exist as good and evil, light and darkness, happy and sad.

Primarily we are going to focus on the two forms of spirit I call "Lower Self" and "Higher Self". Our lower self-vibrates at a lower frequency and vibration than that of our higher self, and because like attracts like, we attract lower vibration people and things into our world. When we are in our higher self we are vibrating on a much higher frequency and vibration and thus attract in high vibration people and things into our perceived world.

The lower self-wants base things, natural things, sex, needs to be met, survival, revenge, and satisfaction. These are not necessarily bad things, some are necessary and part of our physical reality, some are neutral and some are just what they are. But this is where most of the damage occurs to creation.

There can be "lower self" urges that are not "good" such as murder, revenge, or wanting to hurt someone. These are frowned upon by society. We often feel these urges, and though we don't always act on them the key is realizing what you are and what you are not.

A few times in my life I was so angry with someone or so threatened by them that I laid in bed and planned out their murder. I wanted nothing more than make them pay for what they did to me. My lower brain told me how smart I was and how it could get away with the perfect crime. I can't imagine even thinking this way anymore, but at this time in my life, I fought a battle, a battle between my lower self and my higher self. Obviously, my higher self-won as I am not writing this book from prison.

Sometimes we go into victim mode and say "Oh poor me! Look at all the bad things at happen to me." I'm such a nice person why would God do this to me?!"

I am drawn to my higher self, I long to be a better man, but I am human and I do make mistakes. I am getting better loving the part of me that makes mistakes and forgiving me.

Chapter 33
Self-Forgiveness

I struggle to practice self-forgiveness. If you have practiced forgiveness on others I challenge you to take it to the next level and practice it with yourself but don't hate the lower self in the process. Send love and understanding to your mistakes.

John 14:15 If you love me keep my commandments. If we love God what are we doing? What actions do we take? Are we just following a list of rules or are we actively loving people including yourself? Christ replaced the commandments with two, love thy God with all your heart, and love thy neighbor as thyself. To love you is to forgive you.

So you think you have tried self-forgiveness? I want you to try it on a radical level, an unconditional level. Often when I speak to groups of people on my near-death experience I like to ask them a few questions.

Question #1 When you are in your higher self and practicing love or charity such as feeding the homeless or any other selfless service for others, how do you feel about yourself on a scale from 1-10?

Question #2 When you commit a grievous sin, you hurt someone, you stole something, you contemplated murder, or had hate in your heart, how do you feel about yourself on a scale from 1-10?

Most people give themselves an 8 on question 1, and a negative 5 on question 2.

If you answered like the majority of people congratulations! You are human and are stuck in the biggest trap there is; Conditional self-love verging on self-hatred.

I was there most of my life. I would look in the mirror and say, "You are an okay looking man, but if anyone knew what you've done, everyone would hate you as I do." I could not even look myself in the eyes.

I walked around judging myself on my untapped potential. I was an utter failure because I could have been so much more. I focused on the bad things I had done and the things I had failed to achieve.

Can you imagine doing that to your child? Condemning them for not learning to walk at 8 months, for not reading or composing a symphony at age 3, for not being the best athlete or top of their class, or just not forgiving them for making little mistakes. That little child still lives in you. I had to learn to love my little Rabbit, that was my nickname as a child. I had to learn to love and protect that part of me, and not condemn myself for being human. I had to learn to love all of me, both sides of the coin. As long as we focus on what we are not we block what we are.

You are that light, love, and perfection you seek. It is already within you. You just need to stop blocking it and allow it to shine through. You are magnificent and perfect in an imperfect physical form that's purpose is to teach and help our spirit learn.

I think of the parable of the talents Matthew 25:14-30

The master gave each of his servants' talents, one he gave five, one he gave two and the last he gave one. The one who he gave five to, increased it to ten, and the one he gave two to increased it to four, but the one who only was given a small amount he hid it in the ground and was in fear of the master.

This one the master called slothful and wicked. Fear ruled this servant. He was afraid. He didn't count his blessings nor was he optimistic. He expected the master to be hard with him and deal with him in such a manner. The master was more than happy to give us what we want and what we expect we shall receive. When we are in the energy of gratitude and thankfulness we attract more of what we are grateful for. When we focus on our fears and our doubts we attract more of that and become a wicked and slothful servant.

When we focus on what we want and the feeling that good things are coming the Lord grants our desires. We also become more of the light and love that we are when we love and accept our faults but focus on our perfection and what we do want.

What if we are already everything we desire to be? What if it's our nature to be great and it's only fear that stops this process of becoming?

What I desperately wanted I already was. My spirit was strong, my spirit was a protector and defender. My spirit is a warrior, strong confident and powerful. I always pulled for the underdog. I always befriended the friendless. That was the nature of my spirit, the rest was just wrapping paper. Even at my weakest point, my spirit was strong. It was just waiting for me to release the fear. Waiting on me to realize what I was.

One of my heroes is Mr. Rogers. He was not a manly man or a tough guy he was soft spoken and loved children. He devoted his life to making children's lives better. He was often criticized even to the point of vilified.

People blamed him for making a soft generation that everyone was a winner, everyone was loved, everyone was ok just the way they were. No one had to succeed. Everyone was entitled.

I think it's human nature to be competitive. To think we have to beat someone else to win. Mr. Rogers promoted love and acceptance. He never said you didn't have to do anything to be a success. He just said you are loved just the way you are. That sounds a lot like God to me.

If we want to progress we need to work toward our goals, but no matter where we are on our path we are loved. We are perfect and loved. A warrior doesn't want to be just loved, he or she wants to serve, make a difference in their life and others. A warrior doesn't sit back and kick up their feet and do nothing. A warrior understands that faith without works is dead. We are beings of action. If you are not growing you are dying.

Realize you are love and perfect, but work like your survival and the survival of your friends and family depends upon you doing your best. Don't beat yourself up for failing, don't hate the sinner, for the sinner we send love, but we also focus on what we do want. What we want to achieve, what we want differently. How can we make a difference? How can we get this task done?

I think as long as we think we are losers we will stay stuck, but when we send that part love but focus and work toward what we want we will witness miracles. Many professional athletes use this technique. Have you ever seen when a star player makes a mistake? He or she doesn't beat themselves up they take it as a lesson maintains their confidence and get ready for the next play. They don't let the mistake define them. They know who they are. They know they are capable of great things, and they know they are human and prone to mistakes, but they don't let that stop them.

Your spirit is a pro athlete in the spirit realm. Don't let your mistakes made as a human stop you from progressing, you got this, you are confident, you are royalty.

Take your mistakes as learning opportunities. Remember who you are, why you are here for and what you want to overcome and achieve, but also remember you are loved no matter what.

Chapter 34
David and Goliath

David was a warrior for God. He loved God with all of his heart. He wrote psalms and songs about God, his faith was strong. When David was a boy the king of Israel was a man named Saul. Saul and the army of Israel were at war with the Philistines. The Philistines had a champion warrior who stood over nine feet tall his name was Goliath.

Goliath would come to the field of battle and cry in a loud voice challenging the Israelites to battle. *Goliath stood and shouted a taunt across to the Israelites. "Why are you all coming out to fight?" he called. "I am the Philistine champion, but you are only the servants of Saul. Choose one man to come down here and fight me!* **9** *If he kills me, then we will be your slaves. But if I kill him, you will be our slaves!* **10** *I defy the armies of Israel today! Send me a man who will fight me!"* **11** *When Saul and the Israelites heard this, they were terrified and deeply shaken.*

David was a young boy with three older brothers in the army. He was a shepherd and lived with his father Jesse. His father sends him to the war camp with some bread and cheese for his brothers.

David heard Goliath's taunts and asks the soldiers standing near him, *"What will a man get for killing this Philistine and ending his defiance of Israel? Who is this pagan Philistine anyway, that he is allowed to defy the armies of the living God?"*

27 And these men gave David the same reply. They said, "Yes, that is the reward for killing him."

David understood God. David had a relationship with God and he trusted Him with all that he was. David had built this relationship up and saw God defending him against lion and bear attacks on his sheep. David understood faith and God's power. He knew that God was more powerful than a giant that all the soldiers were so afraid of.

His brothers and even the king were incredulous that a boy thought he could take on a giant who was skilled in the art of killing men. They thought that David was foolish or boasting.

What they didn't understand and failed to grasp was the point of me putting this in my book. Everyone thought that they had to rely on their skills to kill the giant that they had to be a better warrior than he was. They missed the point that a warrior for God does not rely on his or her own strength but has unshakable faith because of their relationship with God.

God fights their battles for them.

We all know the story of how David threw a stone in his sling and killed the giant, but the greatest victory David had was turning his heart over to God and trusting him with his life.

Can you imagine trusting God so much that you would go out against a giant that had killed hundreds of men and you were so outmatched in strength that he could easily crush you like a grape? I know at times I have a hard time trusting God with my finances and relationships let alone fighting a Giant.

I question God if He has my back when my income takes a little dip and I worry if it's all up to me. I worry that I am alone and God is indifferent toward me, or I deserve to suffer or not be blessed. Then I read the story of David. I read how much he trusted God. How he went to battle time after time trusting God.

I also love how David sang about God, wrote poems about God, and loved God with all his heart. But the thing I love best about David is that he was human, full of flaws, that he sinned, and lusted after a married woman and even got her husband killed so he could marry her. Don't take that wrong. I don't want to emulate those qualities of David, but I love that he loved God in spite of his flaws and God loved him regardless of his sins.

He recognized God's love for him even though he made mistakes, and because he understood God loved him anyway, David tried a little harder to overcome. David didn't have to be perfect. His actions were flawed but his heart was perfect. He showed he loved God by always turning toward Him and never giving up.

Others around David tried to prove their love for God by keeping the commandments but their heart was not set on God. They didn't trust God the way David did. They were good at the rules but not so good at surrendering their heart to God as David did. They still believed it was up to them and their strength to overcome the enemy.

If our enemy is sin does God expect us to fight the battle based on our strength? Or if we love God as David did and trust God as David did will God fight our battle for us? God shows us through David it wasn't the sin that is the problem but the lack of trust and faith that we are God's.

The best warriors are not the strongest but have the most faith, trust, and deep love for God. Their heart already belongs to God. They may sin, error, and make mistakes, but they always turn and face God and long to be with Him.

Chapter 35
The three stages of Life in being a Warrior.

The first stage is being a victim. Everyone has experienced this in some form or another. This is our lowest vibration, our starting point. Where everything is outside of you, and things happen to you. Where when bad things happen we lament and cry, "Why me?" Where when good things happen, we pat our self on the back or give the credit to God because we are being blessed for being righteous.

This is the stage where judgment abides, where we look and compare. I am smarter than that person, but they are prettier than me. This is where we justify our actions while condemning others. This is where we feel special. Where we "KNOW" we picked the right religion, or we attended the best school and our football team is better than yours.

In this victim stage, we seek approval, and we seek validation. If my sports team is a winner then it makes me a winner. If I am part of an elite circle I have value. If I picked the right and only true religion then I know I will be "saved"!!!! Can I get a hallelujah!? I know I will be given a special place in heaven and most other people will not be.

Even James and John the disciples of Christ asked for a special place in heaven on his left and on his right. Christ chastened them that they did not know what they ask for. He went on to explain, how if you want to be great you must be a minister or servant, even the Son of man came not to be served but to serve and to give his life as a ransom for many.

The first shall be last and the last shall be first. I had a dream once where God showed me who I was before this earth and I saw a multitude of people below us spread out as far as the eye can see. We stood upon a hill and overlooked the multitude. I asked God if I was their leader? I was filled with awe and honored to be in such a position, but God looked at me and said, "No you are their servant." I then saw the vision of me washing each of their feet. I woke from that feeling incredibly humbled. How was I to serve that many, how was I so arrogant to think I was a leader and set apart from others as special?

This taught me to lead is to serve. Great men are not great because they stand on the backs of others, but allow others who are weaker to stand on their backs. To be a warrior is to fight for others, to serve others, and to love others. A warrior can do this because of love, it's not glory that drives him or her, it's not rewards, but a love of service and making a difference. I think Mr. Rogers was a warrior and a hero. He fought for children. He fought for the weakest but held in the highest esteem of God.

As long as we are human we will struggle with being a victim and feeling like it is us against the world, bad or good things happen to us. When this happens, recognize it for what it is. It's our teacher.

In this stage, there is a wide array of vibrations some very low where we lash out and hurt others because we hurt or do selfish things that only serve to feed our inner victim. This is the hardest stage to recognize when you are in it. If accused of being a victim you usually will deny it and maybe even attack the person who accused you of such a terrible thing. We complain about our situation and our life. We suffer from depression and maybe even thoughts of suicide.

There are variations in this stage where we can be succeeding in life and feeling like we are blessed. We can even be a good person serving others and going to church. We can be leaders; we can have many people follow us. We could even be the president of the United States and still be stuck in the victim stage. You probably can name a few politicians who fit in this category.

Question is; Are we in this stage when we judge other for being a victim? It makes me laugh because as long as we are human our programming will automatically kick us into this stage. It takes an effort to recognize our patterns and programming and make a shift into Love.

Our brain is wired and conditioned to automatically shift us to fear and being in victim mentality. This is a survival mechanism. Where things happen outside of us and we have to react to save our lives. Not too many situations in life require the "fight or flight" response. How many times have you been attacked by a bear or a saber-toothed tiger?

We fall into this condition easily. Our brain screams don't trust that person or don't fall in love, remember what happened last time? It turned out terrible!!! Avoid! Run! Shut down! Don't take any risks!

To shift into Love energy and raise our vibration takes more effort. We have to make a choice, an action, and a change. This requires effort on our part.

But what if what happens is bad? What if I caught my partner cheating on me? How can that be my fault? I didn't make them do that. They have their free agency! That is not my fault. I was always faithful and loving, right?

This is still the stage that you believe that things happen outside of our self. It doesn't matter who's at fault. In the scope of how things work on an eternal perspective, this stage is a gift. It's not a bad thing. It is the classroom. It's where we start our learning. It is where some of the greatest lessons in what we are not.

We are love. We have always been love and always been perfect. We chose to experience the opposite, the contrasts, the lessons so we could grow in our understanding and gratitude. When we shift into love and gratitude we can move out of the victim and into the next stage called Creation. I pray that I can love my mistakes but put them aside so I may serve to the best of my ability.

Chapter 36
Creation

The popular book "The Secret" teaches how to create what we want. We are creators. We create our reality. We are powerful; our words have power and magic in them. How we talk to our self, how we think, and feel changes our reality. Our world changes when we change our thoughts and feelings.

How you choose to see yourself with help create your future. I had a blessing from a very in-tune spiritual man and in the blessing, he said that God, Jesus Christ, and the angels held me in very high esteem, that they were present during this blessing and I was noble and great in their eyes. He also said the world saw me differently, not the way God did but viewed me as if I were my sins and saw only the flaws.

This is how I saw myself, as the world saw me. I valued their opinion more than Gods. I believed in the lie, I believed only in my shadow. I kept creating the same pattern, the same results about how I felt about myself.

I was told that I needed to forgive myself and shed the guilt shame and experiences as if they were old garments that should be shrugged off and discarded. I needed to turn to God and put more time and resources into His service.

I have started to grasp some very important concepts into understanding God and what His love means to us. It's not behavior that makes us worthy it's desire and how we keep facing Him when we fall down. It is our intentions coupled with our actions. No matter what we are worthy of love. We can progress and earn blessings based on our creations, this requires work and action along with intention.

Let me restate that, our challenges or how we respond to our challenges do not make us worthy, but rather realizing our challenges can be bigger than us, they can break us and make us fail and only by turning our hearts over to God do we see a victory. He doesn't even require us to overcome the challenge or the sin on our own just the fact that we keep trying and facing Him while loving and forgiving our self is a victory. I believe we need to do our best, be the best creators we can be, but if we fail we need to love all of us.

God loves all of us. He created us with the challenges in the package. I believe that we chose with God what major battles we would face and what major flaws, and sins we would have. We also came with talents and gifts. We are a beautiful coin with two sides. The dark dirty side helps teach us more than the shiny perfect side. It's only through our failures do we really grow. I think I took this to heart at before I came to earth and thought I want to have so much growth if I chose some really hard challenges! It will be fun!! UGH, what was I thinking? I could have had a little less pain and growth and been ok with it.

So, if we are perfect as we are should we be complacent in our flaws, complacent in our sins? I say no that is not who we are. Should we just stay sick because it teaches us what a blessing health is? No, we need to make choices that help our bodies be strong and healthy. We can also choose things that take us on our highest path.

The highest path that you are capable of must be chosen. It is by a thousand little choices do you get closer and closer to the highest path. We need to choose into what we are and not choose what we are not anymore. But this is not a competition. You are not better than anyone else because you have lived a more pure life free from sin, or have made all the right choices. No one knows your path but God. Trust that God has you on the right path as long as your heart is pointed toward Him and not away from Him.

Our thoughts determine how we feel, our feelings determine how we act, our actions determine our results. If you want to change your results change your thoughts. I believe the most important thoughts we have are about us. How you view yourself determines your future.

Act as if it has already happened. One of the most important laws in creation is to set an intention and then act and feel like that intention is already a reality. The Israelites were taught this by the lord in 2 Chronicles 20, Jehoshaphat, the king of the Israelites had to go to battle against three armies. They were severely outnumbered. The people were afraid.

Jehoshaphat prayed to the Lord and was told the Lord would deliver them. Jehoshaphat had so much faith in the Lord that he caused his people to sing songs of praise and thank God for their victory.

The three armies stood to receive and fight the Israelites, but they began to be confused why the Israelites were singing songs of praise for their victory. They hadn't won, they were outnumbered, what was there to sing about? The armies began to contend one against the other. One by one the three armies destroyed each other and the Israelites did not have to fight. God fought for them and let their enemies destroy each other because of their faith and they acted like and felt like God had already made them victorious.

Once they thought they could be and felt that God was on their side, they believed they had already won. When their belief was that solid the laws of the universe had to conspire to fill the vacuum of their belief with what they wanted.

How often do we pray for something and beg for it but in our hearts we are feeling the lack of what we are praying for? We don't pray to God and thank Him for blessing us in advance of receiving it. We are feeling need so the universe gives us need. When we feel blessed the universe gives us more blessings because that is what we are. The laws state that like attracts like and a vacuum must be filled.

When we set our intention and focus on the end result as if it has already happened and give our gratitude for our blessing, the blessing must manifest. It may not do it

in the time we demand, or the way we envision, but it
will happen if you do not lose faith.

As I set my intention and felt the end result, I am
worthy, I am a good man, I started making better
choices. I felt like I deserved good things, I quit
sabotaging myself. I started to create better results.

Chapter 37
Choices

Little choices are the battleground of the warrior. You are a warrior for the light, a warrior for your own path to divine realization. Every day we are faced with choices, from getting out of bed and going to the gym before we go to work or choosing a healthy option to eat instead of something fast and convenient.

You face these choices all the time throughout the day. Most of the time we don't even think about them we just follow a pattern, but the times you feel a choice show up that would forward your progress, pay attention, this is a critical moment

The moment we feel a choice about something we should do we often hesitate, our mind kicks in and starts coming up with excuses. For example, I set myself a goal to work out in the mornings before work. I know if I do this I will have more energy throughout the day and I will lose the extra weight I have been carrying around but I find myself lying in bed coming up with reasons why I shouldn't do it today.

I think I can do it tomorrow, and how tired I am, or how I didn't get a full eight hours of sleep that my body really needs. I end up choosing to stay into bed and I pat myself on my back for choosing what my body needs. I have completely justified my poor choice. I might even start to find other reasons to back up why it was such a good choice even though in my heart I know I sold out. I chose the lower path because the higher path required a choice followed by action.

The lower path requires no action and it's paved with beautiful excuses. I can look back at my path and comment on all the beautiful excuses along my path. I am not financially free because ..... "Fill in the blank" I am not healthy because....., I am not happy because....., I am not in a happy marriage because.....

We have lots of reasons but very few wanted or desired results. We have great intentions but without action, intentions are worthless and empty.

How can we turn those great intentions into results we want? Simple, just don't hesitate jump into the action before your brain has time to sabotage you. Mel Robbins in her book, "The Five Second Rule" teaches us a simple way to stop the hesitation that leads to our sabotage. Mel says when she has a choice in front of her and she feels a hesitation she counts backward from five. 5, 4, 3, 2, 1 Go! When you reach "Go" you do the action that is required to move you forward. She says this changed her life. Changed her finances, her marriage, everything about her life changed because she started using this rule.

People believe that it takes a lot of courage to change, but I want to challenge this. You can be scared and even terrified, just be committed to using this rule. When you feel a hesitation about something you should do that would move you forward in your goal use Mel's rule. 5, 4, 3, 2, 1 Go! Take action.

One of my other favorite things is to set a time and be committed to doing what you say you will do. For example, if it's going to the gym but you really don't feel good, go anyway and touch a machine or walk for any amount of time, just get yourself there. If it's writing your book and you are not feeling the muse, you are not inspired, just show up at the time you set aside, put your hands on the keyboard and type anything. We are creating habits and creating space for things to happen.

If we do anything for long enough it becomes a habit. We are taking action, using small choices to change big things. These small things affect our path. You want more money? Use the rule to take action. Do you need to make phone calls to clients but find yourself resistant to doing it and a million other things take up your day? Use the rule 5, 4, 3, 2, 1 Go! Take action. Make the call. Don't hesitate.

Sounds easy and simple, but fear is what stops us. Fear often cripples us into indecision long enough for our brain to come up with reasons why we shouldn't do the activities that will help us. The countdown doesn't allow your fear to even take form. Your brain is focused on the numbers counting down and we all know what to do when it gets to zero, we blastoff!!!

This is how I finally after years of trying got my book written. I set time aside, set myself a goal to write every day even if it was just a few words, and when the time came to write and I didn't feel like it I counted down and started anyway.

Chapter 38
Warrior Acts

A warrior doesn't think in the critical moment, a warrior acts with conviction.

By refusing to give up her seat to a white man on a Montgomery, Alabama, city bus in 1955, black seamstress Rosa Parks helped initiate the civil rights movement in the United States. She didn't think about it, didn't decide it was time to start a movement, she was tired of giving in, giving up. She said, "I have learned over the years that when one's mind is made up, this diminishes fear; knowing what must be done does away with fear."

So creation can be summed up by setting your intention, feeling like it has already happened, being grateful for the blessing, and when faced with a choice to act, don't think, countdown and do some action.

I promise you if you apply this formula to any area of your life you will watch change and miracles happen.

The next important step to achieve the highest level of this life is to become a divine servant. One of the most important ideals to adopt after learning to become a creator is to learn the lesson of true humility.

Chapter 39
Divine Servant
Humility and Ego

To fully access spirit and God I had to lose my ego, at least put it in timeout. When I have been full of my ego either in feeling powerful and confident or the opposite where I feel like I'm worthless and lower than low, it stems from the ego or the mind trying to compare.

If you are feeling superior to others you are in ego. If you are feeling inferior to others you are in ego. Humility consists of feeling the spirit, connecting, and letting it flow through you without taking ownership of the outcome.

We stay in a pliable state, allowing the spirit to mold and shape us into what it needs us to be. Humility is a very interesting place to be. It's a place where you are all powerful and have the universe at your fingertips yet you don't take the credit for you being amazing. It's a place where you feel you are everything and yet you are nothing. It's a place where you are royalty a son or daughter of the most high God and everything about you is perfect, but our purpose is to serve the lowest of the low. It's a state of duality that mirrors life.

We are powerful and can move mountains and create miracles when we know who we are and where our power comes from. We are the tidal wave when we connect with the universe and we are nothing when we try to stand against the tidal wave. When you understand you are the wave, power and love flow with God's purpose but when you try and be outside of the wave and control the wave we are crushed within its awesome power.

What does the world think of humility? They imagine a person, penniless, living in a wretched state giving everything to the poor and others, taking nothing for oneself. A humble person has nothing or starts from nothing. They are the peasant in the street wearing rags and the opposite of the regal prince who goes by in his fine clothing followed by servants.

Many people strive for humility and end up with false humility where one talks and shows off their humility like they are proud of how humble they are. Both are forms of ego or the mind trying to compare and contrast, rich vs poor, good and bad. What if humility is a duality state of being where you are grateful to God for everything you have and everything you are. What if you are the prince and also the beggar? What if the prince gets out of his carriage and lifts up the beggar feeds and clothes him. What if it is the same being, prince, and pauper? What if you are both at once? Humility is allowing the knowledge of your royalty and position and also your wretchedness to exist at the same time.

Gratitude for everything we have and helps keep us in the state of humility. Practicing gratitude is like building muscles it takes time every day to honor and account for what you have been blessed with.

Realizing that you are both the prince and the pauper at the same time also helps ground us and stay in a true state of humility. That and we are our brother's keeper. We are all one. When you reject someone else you are rejecting a part of yourself. When you love someone else, you are loving a part of yourself.

The true space of humility is the point in-between the two, the prince and the pauper. When you realize your divine nature and your human wretched side and that you are not one, or the other, but both at once. You are a son or daughter of the most high God. You are capable of great things and have the powers of the universe available to you when you realize you are nothing without God. Feel the gratitude for both. I am so grateful for my mistakes and failures and the lessons that they brought in helping me understand my divine nature better. I am so grateful for my body and the opportunity for spiritual growth, and the perspective that it offers. I am so grateful in the compassion being human and making mistakes has granted me for love of others. I am also grateful for the knowledge of my higher self, my divine nature, that I am more than my sinful nature or my mistakes.

God's Ways
Be Open to God and the infinite ways of manifesting.

God doesn't just show up in the way you know as truth. God shows up in many truths and many paths. God is all around you in every rock, in every person, in every molecule throughout the universe. When we reject every other truth but the one we know and understand it is out of ego and having to be right. When we are open and inclusive we recognize God without changing our beliefs but allows others their experience of God.

When someone else's opinion offends us it is because we are afraid of our own doubts. If someone believes differently than you do and you're offended it is because you are not secure in your own belief, and his or her lack of belief scares you. Why do you need them to believe as you do? Their path is not your path. They have had different defining experiences. Their beliefs may be perfect for their path. For you to need others validation for your path means you are not secure in your path. You have doubts. If you are secure in your path you may decide to share what you have found to be true and brings you happiness, but you are not attached if someone else accepts or rejects your message.

Chapter 40
Shadow side

Earlier I told you about God showing me the vision of the coin and how he loved both sides of me. We all have a light side and a dark side of our coin. God didn't love one side of me more than the other, but I sure have. I hated my shadow side, like most good Christians we strive to be better, we shun or sin, hate our sin and only try to be love and light.

Most of my life I hated that I chose sin over God, I hated that I was so drawn to the flesh, the more I tried to stop thinking about sin the more that I thought about sin and how bad I needed it. The more I despised my shadow the more I became my shadow. I would sin and feel bad about it, I would start to believe that something was wrong with me, I was just bad, I was lost. The Mormon scripture "Many are called but few are chosen," played over and over in my head. I was destined for great things, I was one of God's chosen, but I failed, I was to be cast to the wayside. I didn't prove myself worthy of God's exaltation. I wouldn't be chosen. I was not special I was bad.

The more I fought against my shadow the more I became what I hated. It wasn't until I learned from God that He loved both sides of me the same and that I needed to love both sides also. I started practicing self-love and self-forgiveness. It is not an easy thing to do when you have fifty plus years of doing the opposite. I think most people struggle with this.

Is our shadow side evil? I have often asked myself this. I worried about if it was true then was I evil? Was I more evil than good? Would I be weighed by God and if I wasn't overwhelming heavier on my good side I would be put on a crash diet and put in workout hell until I could lose some shadow weight? Is our shadow something to be shunned, ashamed of, and crushed out of existence?

What if we didn't have to worry about it, or be ashamed of it? I know many people will cry blasphemy over this. I have often been called a heretic before. Some people can only believe a certain way and everyone else is wrong. I don't worry about their opinions I only worry about my relationship with God. Am I maintaining a healthy relationship, am I focused on love? What if we focus on what we want instead of what we don't want? What if we look for our light, our highest vibration, and our love? What if all we worry about is becoming love while loving and forgiving our shadow side for the hard lessons it teaches us?

Our shadow side is our teacher. It's not evil or bad. It has a purpose it teaches us contrast. It teaches us the difference between light and dark, love and suffering, saved and lost. We need the shadow side to help define the good. Just like we can never appreciate health without experiencing sickness, or spring without winter, we can't appreciate our light and love without knowing our shadow and fear.

The atonement of Jesus Christ takes care of your shadow side. Oh and not just yours, but everyone's who wants this magnificent gift. It is a gift freely given, no strings attached, nothing asked for in return. It's the ultimate pay it forward gifts. Because we got this awesome gift we want to pay it forward also and share with others the love, and the peace we have found, but guess what? You don't have to pay it forward to keep your gift. You will just naturally want to if you truly value it.

Which brings us back to not focusing on our shadow side. Appreciate and thank it for the lessons you have learned through the process and understand it's purpose of being a teacher of what we are not. If we hate the shadow side we send it energy that it uses to grow. It doesn't care that you hate it, or that you despise its effects. It takes what energy you send it and utilities it. If we send it love and forgiveness it can't help using that to transmute it back into source. Sin was never conquered through hate, sin was conquered through God's infinite love.

Carl Jung, a Swiss psychiatrist, and psychoanalyst who founded analytical psychology contended that *"what you resist not only persists but will grow in size." And today this viewpoint is generally abbreviated to "What you resist persists," with many kindred paradoxical variants—such as, "You always get what you resist."*

So does that mean we should embrace our faults, give up on trying to change, trying to become better? I believe it means, "know thyself." This Ancient Greek aphorism "know thyself" is one of the Delphic maxims and was inscribed in the forecourt of the Temple of Apollo at Delphi.

Know thyself means to understand thyself, both the light and the dark. To understand is to love, to love is to accept and forgive. When we get to the space of self-love and self-forgiveness we reach a state of being where there is no resistance, we get to be and love what we are. Our true nature is free to expand and experience its fullness. We do not focus on the dark, nor the light but accept each part for what it is. The light is our love, the darkness is what defines the light. Without light, there is no shadow, without the shadow there is nothing that defines the light.

In the first book in the Bible, Genesis, God separates the light from the darkness.

> *The First Day*
> 3 And God said, "Let there be light," and there was light. 4 And seeing that the light was good, God separated the light from the darkness. 5 God called the light "day," and the darkness He called "night." And there was evening, and there was morning—the first day...

Before earth, there was no separation of light and dark on the earth or in us. We didn't know or understand one from the other. Think about the letters on this page, they are black surrounded by white. If the letters were white we would get no meaning from reading the page, or it was all black on black, there is no meaning. But when we have either white surrounded by black or black surrounded by white do we gather meaning from the symbols on the page our brain translates into words and meaning.

Knowing oneself requires seeing the contrast and definition between light and dark, lack and abundance, sickness and health, joy and sorrow. Look inside and see what you find. Can you look at yourself without condemnation or judgment? Can you love what you find, both for the good and also for the lessons?

Carl Jung also said, "*Who looks outside, dreams; Who looks inside, awakes.*

> *Everything that irritates us about others can lead us to an understanding of ourselves.*
>
> *Knowing your own darkness is the best method for dealing with the darkness of other people.*
>
> *There is no coming to consciousness without pain.*
>
> *The meeting of two personalities is like the contact of two chemical substances: if there is any reaction, both are transformed.*
>
> *As far as we can discern, the sole purpose of human existence is to kindle a light of meaning in the darkness of mere being.*
>
> *We cannot change anything until we accept it. Condemnation does not liberate, it oppresses.*

Carl Jung was a great teacher and understood the shadow's side and purpose and how to shine the light on our purpose being here.

My salvation came in self-forgiveness for not condemning myself for having a shadow side; a side that came with built-in sins. When I finally learned to start loving me as a whole, I started to change. I understood I could accept the atonement of Christ.

When I condemned and hated my shadow side I gave it energy and it could grow. When I accepted and loved it for what it was, my teacher, I could focus on what I did want and what I did love, not on what I felt bad about and thought I should change because of shame. When I focused on what I did want that was given energy and it could grow and expand, while my shadow was loved but not given attention and it started to shrink. The shadow side didn't care what kind of attention or energy it was given it could feed of either as long as it was given energy and attention.

The shadow side of humanity gives the light side the opportunity to become more compassionate, the ability to step up, serve and make a difference. If bad things didn't happen we would never have inspirational people who sacrificed and made a difference that changed the world.

Some of the greatest heroes the world has known were thrust into a situation that was born from the shadow. Mahatma Gandhi, Rosa Parks, Martin Luther King, and William Wallace are great examples of the light side being defined by the shadow. Racism, abuse, genocide, murder, and all the other horrible things that happen in life gives the light a chance to shine. These are examples of the shadow outside of yourself, but it is the same on the inside. We can witness our shadow love and forgive and become the light, the love and teach the lesson. Shine love and compassion, equality, and joy when the teacher shows up. Take the teacher for what it is, something that defines the light, and be the good. The heroes didn't just complain about the injustice of their situation, they made a difference. They focused on what they could do to change things for the better. They chose something hard and focused on what they wanted not on what they didn't want.

Life can be set up in two camps; The "don't want" and the "do want" camps, the working behaviors, and the non-working behaviors. One side we are focused on what we want to create and what is working for us, and the other side is what we don't want and what isn't working.

If we spend our focus, time, and efforts in the don't want and non-working areas of our life we stay stuck and we create more of what we don't want and what isn't working. When we learn the lessons the dark side of the equation taught us and focus on what is working toward our do wants we see miracles happen. The path of our life is like a trail through the woods. On each side of the path are brambles that sometimes have big sharp thorns. As we stray off our path and we are caught in the brambles we experience pain and suffering. The brambles are a gift to let us know when we are off the path. The shadow side is to teach us and guide us from being what we are not and keep us on the path of what we are.

193

Chapter 41
Fear is the enemy

Fear can take over, cripple us, keep us from moving forward, cause doubt about everything and remove us from love.

A warrior for God feels the fear and sends it love and light. A warrior thanks fear for the lesson. A warrior understands fear is a teacher.

A victim lets fear control them, cripple them, and points blame at everything but the source and creator of the fear, which is their own mind.

A warrior accepts he or she has created the fear in their mind, therefore, they have the power with God to dissolve it.

I recently went through a very dark time in which fear not only controlled and crippled me but actually sought to take my life. I felt the only way to beat the fear was to die. In the short time, it controlled me I was in the darkest place of my life. Every day seemed like my last. I didn't know how I could make it one more day. I thought if I keep having these panic attacks I will be forced to kill myself just to make it stop. I kept hearing a voice in my head saying the only way to make the panic attacks stop was to die.

Family and friends counseled me to go to my doctor and get some help, but that idea seemed stupid. My mind found many ways that wouldn't work. It cost too much money if I was a man I could stop it, I didn't need someone else's help, it would take years to overcome this, I didn't want to take drugs to numb my mind, and the list went on and on.

In this way, fear was protecting itself. It didn't want to die. It wanted to isolate me. Keep me from talking to my friends, family, and any professionals. I was embarrassed I was having these panic attacks also and thought if I am this tough warrior I shouldn't feel fear. It was a deficiency in me that was causing these attacks. If I was brave I wouldn't feel scared. Admitting I was scared made me feel less of a man, less of a warrior at the time. A warrior for God is humbled and knows his strength comes from God not is own willpower or muscles.

Obviously, it was a prime example of another way I had failed. I couldn't even be brave anymore. I was a coward. I should die. It caused me to feel even worse about myself, which caused me to feel more like a failure, which caused more fear.

I had some bad circumstances that helped trigger the panic attacks, but that was not the root cause, only a symptom of what was going on inside my head. I had moved from self-love to self-hatred.

I got on my knees and begged God for a sign, an answer to the question if He still, needed me if He wanted me to write my book. I wondered if I was even still worthy to write this. Wouldn't anyone want to hear a message about God from someone as broken, weak and sinful as I am? I am still a messenger? Can a messenger be as flawed as me, still have an effect on people? Would I still be a profitable servant?

I prayed and prayed to God, begged him for a sign. I was listening to a good book about an NDE called, "Dying To Be Me" by Anita Moorjani. I was listening to the part that God created miracles in getting her message out. Dr. Wayne Dyer contacted her and asked to help her write and publish her book. I was blown away and inspired. I thought if this is God's book I'm writing, He will help me not only get it out but He will help pull me out of this dark pit I have fallen into. He will pull me out and I will be able to write again.

I paused the audiobook and got onto my knees. I begged God for some help, I begged Him to send an angel to help me. I begged Him that I would see an angel and they would give me a message. The angel would confirm You want me to write this, that I am worthy, that I have a message You want me to deliver.

I waited and looked at the ceiling. I looked around the room. I anticipated the ghost of Dr. Dyer would materialize and give me a message of hope and that God was on my side and I had an important message. I waited and looked and waited some more. Nothing. I got crickets… just crickets.

I was crushed. Why didn't God answer my prayer? I didn't get my angel, not even a still small voice. Not a peep!!! I was desperate. I yelled at the sky, "God you said if your son asks for bread, would you give him a stone?" quoting the scripture from the bible. I yelled, "Yes, apparently you will! Here Ryan here is a mouthful of stones! I hope you choke on that! That's what I get. I get stones!"

I was furious with God for the first time in a long time. I had always taken what was thrown at me with the attitude of "I trust my Father" and I would move forward with faith, but not this time. I was done! "Screw all of this," I shouted. "I am so #$#%@ done! I am done telling people about You. You will just disappoint them and make them feel forsaken too! You don't care!! I started to cry and felt nothing but darkness and fear. I was so lost, so ready to die. I was done at the end of my rope. I had no gas left in the tank, nothing to compel me forward. I was completely without hope. I so longed for death, and I wanted to kill myself, but I just couldn't. I couldn't leave my granddaughter Max. She was the only good thing left to me.

I kept having panic attacks, so severe with fear as intense as night in Antarctica. It froze my heart and yet it raced over 200 beats per minute. I couldn't breathe. I felt like I was losing my mind and I would always be in the grip of this intense fear.

I bought some CBD oil and started taking it. It helped make the panic attacks less intense and less frequent. I tried not to think about anything that would upset me or trigger a panic attack, but sometimes worrying that I might have a panic attack would trigger one. I worried that I would be this way forever. It was like a monster was waiting just at the edge of my vision. I knew it was there and if I turned my head and looked at it in the face it would rush forward and seize me by the throat. That is how the panic attack felt. I just couldn't acknowledge it.

It seemed like my life was spinning out of control. I was fired from my job of 8 years. I broke up with my girlfriend.

197

My health was questionable with kidneys shutting down and liver problems. It was like everything that could go wrong was going wrong. Financially, health, emotional, and my love life, everything was bad and out of my control. I think when things got bad with my girlfriend is when the panic attacks started.

I was afraid I was losing everything and everything in life was turning against me. I heard false untrue rumors on why I was fired from my job. An employee that worked there was telling people I got fired for child porn. This was an absolute lie, but some of my friends believed it. I was crushed and shattered. How could people think this about me? Don't they know me?? I wondered. I complained to some of my friends who did have faith in me, "Don't they know if this was true, the company would have had to call the police? Are they that stupid they didn't think about that? Of course, it wasn't true or I would be in jail." I felt like my reputation had been smeared and damaged beyond repair.

This wasn't the first time I was accused of doing something horrible and untrue. Every time it was an attack by the enemy and I felt my life was over if people believed these horrible rumors about me my mission was over, I had no purpose. I was only here to serve God and make a difference. If Satan could get people to believe terrible things or more importantly if he could discourage me, I would take my own life and my mission would be thwarted.

The thing I was forgetting, every single time I had been falsely accused the truth would eventually come out. God protected me and I was always vindicated. I had a person who had accused me of things on social media ended up calling me a year later and apologizing and blaming their behavior on being bi-polar. I was in God's hands but it was hard to trust and remember that when you are in the midst of tribulation.

It seemed like God was throwing me to the wolves. The last time everything went bad He took my favorite dog, Snoop, who I still desperately miss. I wondered what was next, was I going to lose someone I loved again? I felt I couldn't take much more.

The next morning after I had pleaded with God to send me a message and take away my panic attacks, I had the worst morning as far as panic attacks. I had four severe attacks by two in the afternoon. I was at my wits ends and I continued to pray for deliverance.

My deliverance came in the form of a text. I got a message from a woman from my past that I had a relationship with. We dated and then she got married. I hadn't seen her in about a year. She said she had to see me. I was curious about what she wanted.

I agreed to meet her at Barnes and Nobel in SLC. I drove down filled with anticipation. What did she want? I got there early and walked into the store looking for her. I was filled with anticipation and wonderment; was she here? I scanned every aisle and determined she hadn't gotten there yet. Would she show? Did she chicken out? I looked at my watch every few seconds trying to guess when she would get there.

I looked up from my watch and she was walking toward me. My heart and my stomach switched places and then back again. I was nervous and wondering what she wanted. I was dating my girlfriend and she was still married. I hadn't even told my girlfriend the truth about going down to meet her. She gave me a shy nervous smile as she approached and said Hi in her soft voice.

I tried to hug her and she walked away and said follow me. We sat down and she told me there isn't a day that goes by she doesn't think of me. "But that's not the reason I came here." She said. "I am not going to leave my husband and we can't talk or have anything that looks like an affair. I am choosing my family still. I can't break my family up just to be happy. I don't know what God has in store for us, but it's not now."

I sighed a big breath out. I sure didn't want to be the reason for a broken family or a divorce and I didn't want to upset my girlfriend but I was curious if she still loved me I was insatiable and no matter how much my girlfriend loved me it wasn't enough because I was despising myself right then. I mumbled my agreement and asked, "Well, why are you here? Why did you ask to see me?"

She looked deeply into my eyes and asked, "Where are you in writing your book? I have a message from God that you need to finish it. People are waiting desperately to read your story. You can help so many people."

I looked at her with shock and bewilderment. I had my answer. I had a visit from the angel I begged God to send me. She was flesh and blood but I couldn't imagine someone who would shock and inspire me more to write. An angel that came to deliver a message and then leave, someone I didn't expect, from another state, from my past who I had respect and wanted to impress. She was inspired to deliver a message to me from God. I knew God had not forsaken me. I knew I was in His hands and that He allowed me to have the experience of pain and suffering of what I had allowed or created. He sent the one person I wouldn't reject their message. Everyone else close to me including my girlfriend would have given me the same message and I would have rejected it.

I realized that pain is inevitable. This life is full of both joy and pain. We can't live and not experience pain, but suffering is optional. The story we make up in our head about how unfair this is, or we can't take anymore, or whatever we tell our self that is what creates suffering. If I can feel the pain but know I am in God's hands, know that it will be ok I don't have to suffer. I can feel pain but have peace.

God offers us His peace. He loves us and helps us with what we need and ask for, but not always what we want or how we think He should answer our prayers. God answered my prayer in a much different manner than I thought He would, but it was perfect.

I felt an energy change in my being. I felt hope, peace, and purpose fill me again. I think for me the most important key was to get my purpose back. I am only here to be a divine servant. Every time I try to control the outcome, live selfishly or expect things I am disappointed. When I allow God to operate in the manner that already is and is the correct way, I find peace and things work out perfectly. When I try to control the situation I am always disappointed and suffer.

I had suffered so much, so deeply that I was ready to take my own life, end things right then and there. I was positive I couldn't go on. What miracle happened that changed things? Did an angel come down from heaven and with a trumpet shout out that I was God's servant and I hadn't been forsaken that I had a purpose and God loved me? No, that's what I wanted but God chose another way to show me, a way I didn't expect.

He uses us as His messengers and angels. You can be a messenger and an angel to someone right now if you are open to listening to the promptings in your heart. Are you open to serving God, being His angel to someone else? Are you open to having human angels deliver the message your soul longs to hear?

My suffering was so deep that when I allowed God in to fill the space that the pain had carved out in my soul, love peace and immeasurable joy flooded in. I went from being miserable to having a deep love for everyone around me, a peace and stillness in my soul, a powerful feeling of contentment. I looked at life through new eyes. Situations that caused me pain before seemed trivial.

I was looking for an outside influence to make me feel loved, and on the path. I didn't realize that I had the answers within and that God is my source. I am His servant. When I can trust Him with everything, it seems to work out way better than when I try to be in control.

Surrender equals peace, but only if you have trust in whom you are surrendering to. I didn't trust God so I couldn't surrender. I didn't know if I had done something to make God turn his back on me if I had taken too long to write this book, and He had given up on me. I thought I was a failure. I didn't look back on all the times God had my back, how many times He protected me, shielded me, and kept me alive. My judgment was skewed. I could only see the problem in front of my face.

Trust is built. It requires interaction, history, and proof that the other person is trustworthy. You can't trust someone you just met, you may have faith that things will turn out good or you can follow your gut, but trust is built on a history of interaction. Do we cultivate that interaction with God? Are we building that relationship of trust and remembering what God has done for you? Are we allowing God the space to show us He loves us and He is protecting us and we are dear and special to Him? Or are we demanding and not trusting that He will deliver in the way we want and demand. God is not the genie in the lamp or our servant that must meet our demands, but I have acted like He is at times. I demanded things of God because I didn't trust His way. I had failed to look back at the evidence and trust He had built with me.

I was asking God for a scrap of bread to show me that I could trust Him. I thought He was giving me stones because He didn't answer my prayer the instant I prayed it. God gave me my answer and it wasn't a scrap of bread, it was a full meal. It was the fatted calf. Just like in the prodigal son, my Father ran to me when I was most broken, He killed the fatted calf and gave me a feast. He clothed me in His finest robe. All because I was humble enough to ask for forgiveness, beg for His help, and walk the way home. I wish I could write how much faith I had and how well I did in trusting God and I could be a shining example on how to show God I trust Him, but we both know that's not true. I am a broken, fail-able human being that God had to take the shattered pieces and makes something new out of.

The reality was once I surrendered to God and gave up the struggle of trying to control the things happening in my life, my natural state of being "joy and bliss" could shine through. Life causes us to wear a mask of what "we are not". The mask is a teacher and provides contrast, but we are not the mask. We are the joy and the bliss behind the mask. Our nature is love.

To get to the state of bliss mankind has tried so many things, prayer, meditation, religion, doing good, denial of self, and many other things. While those can be very effective we also need to surrender and be in a state of reminder. Remind yourself to surrender, remind yourself that you are love. Forgive yourself for wearing the mask. Forgive yourself for learning what you are not. Forgive and love yourself, realize you are the love, not the lesson. It requires work and effort to stay in surrender but if we want that feeling of bliss, it is worth the effort.

When you are love that's all you want to be. We can't imagine doing something that is not loving. We can't imagine hurting someone else or doing something outside of our character. Conversely, when we are wearing the mask and we don't feel worthy, or we are not enough, we seek things to reinforce those feelings. We find ways to sabotage our self. We find ways to create suffering.

Even when things seem clear and we make a change old programming in our brain takes over and we have a tendency to slip back into old patterns. The trick to change your life into what you want is to first have a vision of how you want your life to look living your highest self. Hold that vision in your mind every day by putting up reminders like pictures, quotes, and watching motivational videos or clips. Try to stay in the positive energy every day.

I was looking for a way to stay in the state of bliss that God put me in a few days ago, but which seemed to be slipping out of my grasp a little day by day. Writing seemed to help and focus me on my goal of being one of God's messengers, but feelings of inadequacy and unworthiness kept creeping in. I could feel myself looking toward my addictions for relief from the stress, but I knew that wouldn't help other than a quick fix that only lasted a short time.

I decided to get back into the habit or my success and gratitude journals. Every night I write a list of what I am grateful for in my life. I put the obvious things like my kids and my health, and especially my granddaughter, but I also try to dig deep and think of things that I haven't thought of or appreciated in a while. When I finish what I am grateful for I start on my success journal and I write about what I accomplished today. Success breeds success and feeling that good energy attracts more of the same tomorrow. I talk more about this at the end of this book.

I am grateful I can write this book that may help someone who is feeling the same way I did. I want you to know that I love you and appreciate you taking your time to read my book. I pray that it may touch you and uplift and inspire you. You are an amazing person who has a great spirit and purpose so don't forget it.

Chapter 42
7 Rules I learned from God to guide my life.

After my NDE I began to understand a few things relating to the other realm or the spiritual side of this life. Probably the most basic and fundamental rule of life is, we are love. We are a perfect expression of love. We came to the physical realm to realize this more fully, and the only way to fully experience love is to also know what it's not and remember what we are.

RULE #1: We are perfect expressions of love expressed in an imperfect manner.

Rule #2: Time does not exist outside of this realm. We are moving through time in this life, but on the other side we can move anywhere through time, forward, back, sideways, there are no limitations. Everything is the now.

Rule #3: Pain is part of this life, but suffering is optional.

Rule #4: The highest expression of love we can achieve is the Divine Servant

Rule #5: Fear is the enemy to peace, but it is also the teacher. Memories hold on to fear and form our reality. To clear this we need to clean and clear our memories through love.

Rule #6: Know thyself, thy "whole self" the light and the darkness. Love both sides of the coin.

Rule #7: What we understand the nature of God to be is our limitation. What our minds hold as beliefs and truths, is the framework of our limitations. The details of our limitations are based in memory and experience. This makes up our limiting truth.

Rule #1 We are perfect expressions of love expressed in an imperfect manner.

I love my granddaughter more than I love anything in this world. She is two and a half. She is pure love. She lives with me and when I get home from anywhere she hears me come in and screams, "PAPA!!!" at the top of her lungs and runs full speed into me as she throws her arms around me. I have never felt so loved or felt such a pure love outside of God.

Conversely, when she gets upset or hurt, watch out! She fell off the couch today I was working on my computer with my back to her. I heard her fall and she started to cry. I turned around and asked her if she was ok in my most loving grandpa voice. She looked at me with pure anger and screamed at me and started to pick up the closest things to her, which were the couch pillows and throw them at my head. She threw pillow after pillow at me while screaming in rage. She ran off and I went back to work on my computer. Suddenly I started to get wet. She found a spray bottle and started spraying me in the head. I turned around and saw anger wearing her face as a mask. She genuinely wanted to hurt me and she was acting out because she got hurt.

How can someone who loves me so much one minute be so angry with me the next even when it's not my fault she got hurt? I just happened to be the person closest to she could lash out at. How often as adults do we act like toddlers and lash out at someone even though we are angry about something else?

Every conflict every misunderstanding comes from an imperfect expression of love. We are love and we get hurt and we lash out because we want to be loved and understood.

My youngest son Alex when he was about five years old, wanted to play with his older brother who was about fourteen and my son's friends. Sean, my oldest, has his two best friends Dillon and Jeff over. They were watching TV and Alex was pestering them to play with him. They told him to go away so Alex picked up his Fisher Price plastic golf club and began to hit Dillon in the back and head with it, while screaming at him, "I just want you to be my friend!"

Jeff and Sean were laughing so hard at poor Dillon taking a beating from a five-year-old. Dillon pleaded his case by saying over and over "I am your friend! Stop hitting me!" Alex wouldn't stop until I took the golf club away and sent him to his room.

Be my friend, love me, how often do we mean that when we are in a fight with someone we love that has hurt us. If we could remember they are also imperfect expressions of love trying their best maybe we would be less quick to anger and less quit to assume they are trying to hurt or offend us.

When you can set your hurt aside and give them the benefit of the doubt that they are crying out for love also and try to understand why they are hurt or offended many conflicts could be avoided.

Remember we are all imperfect expressions of the love we are and the love we crave. Very few people are malicious or evil. Most are crying out for love in a really messed up way. How can we reach those people and help them know we want to listen and understand why they acted the way they did. It is a difficult thing to do to set aside your own hurt and love someone who has hurt you, but it is one of Christ's most important teachings. Love those that despise you. How can we love someone more than trying to understand why he or she is acting out? Why they are imperfectly expressing their love? Their love is perfect; their expression needs some work, maybe a lot of work.

It's good for me to think, "Wow someone else may be more messed up than even me. If I need love maybe they do too."

Rule #2: Time does not exist outside of this realm. We are moving through time in this life, but on the other side we can move anywhere through time,

forward, back, sideways, there are no limitations. Everything is the now.

Time on the other side or in Heaven does not exist. There is only the now. Everything happens in the now. Time was created by God, for man to experience the physical realm. When God showed me my life in heaven I saw everything as it happened in the blink of an eye. I experienced everything again as if it was happening but from God's perspective, not mine. I saw everything as a beautiful lesson that helped me grow and learn.

We experience time in a linear manner. Time passes by second by second, minute by minute, and hour by hour. Time is experiential, meaning we have no reference for what time is until we experience it. You are very familiar what a day feels like, but have you ever experienced a day where you slept it away or it seemed to pass so quickly and others that seemed to take forever to get over. When we are ten years old one year is one-tenth of your life. It is a big or long period of time-based on your experience. When you are eighty years old the same amount of time one year or three hundred and sixty-five days are only one-eightieth of your life. It is fractionally a lot smaller or quicker period of time based on your experience. This is why it feels like time speeds up as you age.

Time is also based on your perception. Time flies when you are having fun, but when you are bored the minutes seem to slowly tick away at a snail's pace. I have experienced days I wanted to end very quickly but they took forever and others I wanted to last forever but they were gone in the blink of an eye. Think about working at a boring job versus being on the beach in Hawaii. Which one ends faster?

Our physical bodies are stuck in this time frame because of the limitations our mind and our beliefs create the framework of our reality. We believe time is a constant. It is a fact and it can be measured. We have experienced time pass and never have seen anyone travel through time. And if we heard a story of a man being two places at once, or moving through time we would immediately suspect a trick, a hoax, or at worst a charlatan.

I found this story on the internet about Sai Baba.

There was an Indian Swami named Sri Sathya Sai Baba. He inspired millions and have devotees and followers all over the globe. He performed miracles like materializing a Rolex watch out of thin air.

Once Swami Sai Baba picked up a South African devotee for the interview. This devotee was full of doubts about Baba and it was the first time he came to Parthi with an intention to understand Baba.

After talking to him for a while Swami asked him what do you want? The man replied, "I want a watch." Baba immediately materialized a watch and gave it to him. The man asked further that He wanted a bill of sale. Well, Swami waved His hand in the thin air to give a bill, which, to the astonishment of the devotee had the address of his hometown in South Africa, with that day's date. Totally surprised the devotee took that invoice and came out of the room wondering how on earth could Swami buy a watch from his own town which was more than 10,000 miles away from Parthi and produce a bill in advance of him asking for it.

On his return to his town, he went to the shop, which issued the invoice, to find the duplicate of the invoice. It was there. No magic, he held the duplicate of the invoice up to the original he held. The shop owner recollected the incident and narrated "On that, the invoice was written, a small tiny person with curly hair and red robe came into my shop to buy a watch. He spent a long time to select this one on your wrist and, paid the money. He immediately left the place but after a few minutes he came back into the shop and asked for a receipt. He was a very pleasing personality and a good customer, the shopkeeper remembered.

After reading this, skeptical part of my brain wants to figure out how this was faked, and it had to be a hoax, but after what I experienced in heaven it makes me wonder. What if it was real, what if we are capable of far more than the mundane average lives we live.

Time for us is a constant because our belief system is firmly grounded in evidence that time is real and it cannot be moved through, stopped, or traveled. Why are so many books, movies, and stories about time travel? Why are we so obsessed with it if it cannot be changed? I think it's because our spirits remember the other side. God has the ability to alter time, change our reality. I had a very sacred experience with this where the Lord rewound time. I was told I cannot write about the experience, but I can say that the Lord changed what happened and showed me that he will alter our experience in time if it suits the greater purpose.

There are many things we don't understand nor may we ever understand them but I do know that God does know Alpha to Omega and He is outside of time. He knows our whole life. There is not anything we can do to surprise Him, disappoint Him, anger Him, or have Him feel anything but love for us.

Rule #3: Pain is part of this life, but suffering is optional.

Eckhart Tolle tells the story of a duck in his book _A New Earth_. In the story, the duck gets into an intense altercation with another duck. They fight violently for a few seconds and then separate. As the ducks part, each makes a great show of shaking its feathers and wings. In an instant, all their anger and intensity is released. The conflict ends and all goes back to normal; no more pain, no more suffering. The ducks don't hold a grudge against each other.

In addition to an opposable thumb, humans are also different from animals because of our consciousness. Our minds hold memories and interpret what's happening right now as the worst thing that can happen; it projects visions for the future all that looks like worst case scenarios. Our extraordinary minds allow us to live far outside the reaches of our present moment and circumstances. Because of this, we get the opportunity to relive and sensationalize the negative events of our past and anticipate catastrophic misfortune in our future.

213

I love the Buddhist quote, "pain is inevitable, but suffering is optional." The damage we do to ourselves in our minds often far exceeds that of the actual events. I love the story of two Buddhist Monks. One is the master and one is a student. Monks are supposed to be celibate. They cannot even touch a woman let alone be married to one. One day the two monks are walking through a village that had suffered from a great flood.

The monks come across an old woman trapped on the wrong side of the swollen river. The master waded across the river picked up the old woman and carried her across the river set her down and continued on his way. The student walked behind the master in shock. His master had broken an important rule! He was mortified. He thought about it all day as they walked finally he couldn't take it anymore and burst out, "Master, why did you carry that old woman?" The old master looked at the young monk and said, "What are you talking about?

The young monk was so upset he shook with frustration and shouted we are not supposed to touch women; you carried that old woman across the river! The old monk said, "Ahhhhh, I see. Yes, I carried her across the river but you have carried her all day."

How long do we carry our problems in our minds? How long do we worry needlessly over something that may not even happen? Or stew and think about how someone has wronged us or what we've lost. I have found a few things that help me get out of suffering and get out of the pattern in my mind.

Take Action:

Get up do something productive, keep your hands busy and your mind will not dwell on what is causing you to suffer. If you can find an action that will lead to a solution that is even better, but doing something even if it's going for a walk or doing some chores will keep your mind occupied. If your mind has nothing to keep it occupied it will find things to solve or worry about.

How to take action: When you feel you need to do something and you don't immediately act on it, your mind will start coming up with excuses on why you shouldn't take action. Do the countdown 5,4,3,2,1 blastoff and take action without thinking or giving your mind a chance to tap out.

Head to the gym, go for a walk, start on a project, just get yourself doing something that will move you forward.

Boxes:

When I am worried about one area of my life such as if you had a bad day at work don't bring the energy home to poison the home life. Put it in a box that you can revisit it tomorrow. It will still be there for you to pick and worry about it another time; do not steal the joy from other areas of your life.

If you have to pull your car over on the way home from work and scream at the top of your lungs, pound your fists on the steering wheel, and throw a tantrum, do it! This will release some energy that is bottled up inside and allow you to put it in a box to deal with it later.

Just because you picked up a can of stinking garbage at work doesn't mean you come home and pour it out over your kitchen table for everyone else to enjoy the stench. You wouldn't do this with real garbage but we do it all the time with mental garbage.

Deal with the energy of it as a duck does, shake it off and go about your business.

Perspective:

Our perspective on problems can make something bigger than it is or smaller depending on how you choose to see it. This is a really big area of our life. Our brains are wired to shift us to the negative.

Just imagine your goal is across the room from you. You set your mind on reaching that goal. You are excited to reach this goal your eye is set on it and you have a singular focus. As you walk across the room you walk into a chair that is in the middle of the room you hadn't seen. You stumble across it hurting your shin. You take your eyes off the goal on the other side of the room to look at what you hit.

It's a chair. You kneel down and examine the chair closer. You have to figure out how to get around this chair. You examine it from every side, you look closer and closer until your vision is consumed with the chair; you can't even see your goal anymore, all you see is chair.

This is how we deal with problems we focus on them until all we can see is the problem. If we could take a step backward we could see the chair isn't that big in fact we could step around the chair easily and continue to our goal.

What we focus on expands. When you are focused on the problem instead of the goal we lose sight of our goal and the problem becomes everything. When we step back from the problem and refocus on our goal and what we need to do to keep moving toward it, the problem becomes less large.

We have two theaters in our brain where a movie is constantly playing. One is the fear theater and the movie is always fear based and how we must protect our self from the worst thing that can happen. The other is the love theater where we feel joy and peace and we look at others and our self through the eyes of love. When you look at things from a love perspective it changes whatever you are looking at as a lesson or something positive. When we are in the fear theater the same thing can look scary and dangerous.

To get to the love theater we must take action and make a choice to switch to love. Our switch to the fear theater is automatic. One little thing can trigger us into fear and we have to make a conscious choice and put in effort to switch our perspective back to the love theater.

This takes practice but the more often you do it the better you will get at it, and the less often will you be triggered into fear.

4-Meditate

I come out of meditation with such clarity and focus, and often have new solutions to problems and strategies that allow me to deal with the challenges I'm facing. Find a way to meditate, even if it's only for 5 to 10 minutes a day. It is life-changing.

5-Practice Gratitude

Do your success journal and gratitude journal once a day. This helps program your brain for success. The more you focus on what blessings you have and what you have been able to accomplish the more you will attract that is of the same energy. Practice not complaining, complaining actually wires the brain for negativity and attracts more of what you don't want into your life.

Gratitude 10 things	Success Today 10 Things
1 Max love that little girl	1 Wrote!
2 My health	2 Exercise
3 Clear mind	3 Gratitude and Success Journal
4 Beautiful weather	4 Connected with friends
5 Good friends	5 Self-care
6 Kids who love me	6 Found 4 opportunities to be kind
7 My Father in Heaven	7 Found ways to be service to others
8 The Atonement	8 Ate healthy food
9 Nature	9 Read uplifting books/scriptures
10 My message	10 Took time to enjoy life

6-Pray

Prayer is a powerful way to connect to your higher power and higher purpose. There is something magical about putting our thoughts into words and speaking them. In Genesis, the Lord said, "Let there be light and there was, and He saw that it was good." Speaking the words helps our thoughts and prayers to manifest in the physical realm. Voicing our concerns and our hopes and being thankful to our higher power creates miracles, and the more people we have praying with one purpose the more things are changed for the better.

I was told in a blessing if I was humble and prayerful no good thing will be withheld from me. I believe that is true for all of us. If we reach out to God and pray to Him we are creating a relationship.

7-Exercise

This is a key area for your overall growth. Mind, Body, Spirit, Social, and Business need to be balanced to have a happy healthy life. Too many people say that they are too busy to exercise; Zig Zigler said he was too busy to not exercise. I love that. When you prioritize your time and take time to appreciate and take care of the wonderful body you have been given, the dividends will pay handsomely. I notice when I work out my mind is clearer, my stress levels are down and I feel more energized.

8 – Connect with Others

There may be nothing as rejuvenating as a stimulating conversation with another human being. When we feel bad, it is easy to isolate ourselves and not ask for help from others. This is not for everyone some people who are introverts need alone time while others feel better and more connected when they can talk with someone who cares and will listen to them.

I try and surround myself with coaches, mentors, and role models. When I need advice from someone on business I have friends and mentors I can call when I need relationship advice I have friends who have navigated tricky situations and found ways to compromise. You become the people you associate with so why not surround yourself with amazing people you admire.

9-Listen to Music

One of the most amazing gifts we have to connect to our soul with is music. Music has been shown through research to take your mind off your troubles, ease the pain, make you feel connected and energized. Music is a key to our emotions, it unlocks how we feel, it can bring us to tears, inspire us or bring up a depth of feelings we didn't know was in us.

Rule #4: The highest expression of love we can achieve is the Divine Servant

We talked a little about becoming a divine servant earlier in the book, and about humility and ego, and being both the prince and the pauper.

When we are in the service of our fellow beings we are in the service of our God. When you lose yourself in service you find yourself. The fastest way to happiness to take the focus off of your life and put in on others. The most fulfillment we can have is when we feel we are a benefit to other people. We have a purpose in life because we give service.

Rule #5: Fear is the enemy to peace, but it is also the teacher. Memories hold on to fear and form our reality. To clear this we need to clean and clear our memories through love.

The best example of how to do this is the Hawaiian art of forgiveness called "Ho'oponopono" is a Hawaiian practice of reconciliation and forgiveness. The Hawaiian word translates into English simply as correction, with the synonyms manage or supervise, and the antonym careless.

How I like to describe the practice is this: Your neighbor steals your pig. You know he did it and rather than having the anger consume you with injustice and you being wronged, you forgive him in a radical way. You go to your neighbor and say, "I am sorry. Please forgive me. I love you. Thank you."

I am sorry I didn't see if you needed anything or was in need of a pig. Please forgive me for not being my brother's keeper and checking up on you or expecting you to be in a place that stealing would seem like a wrong thing to do. Let me help you. I love you. You are my brother. Thank you for teaching me this valuable lesson on love and forgiveness."

There are deeper levels of this concept past just forgiving your neighbor or those that have wronged you. The deeper you go into forgiveness you realize you have to forgive you. That you are the creator of your life, forgive your neighbor but also forgive yourself in the part of it that you created.

What if everything that happens in your life was all part of your "game"? I was doing a meditation on the archangel Metatron because I had read something about him and I wanted to know who he was. I had options I could go to the internet and see what other people have said about him or I could ask him myself.

I felt like I was in a good space to receive answers so I meditated on him and when I was feeling very deep and still, I called him by name and asked him who he was. I immediately felt warmth and love and I heard, "I am in charge of the code." I asked what is the code? He answered, "Let me put it in a way that you can understand.

Your life is a video game. It was designed by you and God to create the perfect learning experience and provides the maximum amount of growth. You came here to learn. Everyone and everything you come into contact with is part of your game. Everyone is there to support your learning. You are playing a character with built-in talents and flaws but is not you, you are something more, something infinite and perfect. I weave others games into your game so you can both learn from each other. You get to choose and you get to experience those choices, but this does not define you, only teach you. Some of what you learn is what you are not and some of what you learn reminds you about what you are. You are love experiencing life in the physical form.

So if we are playing a role or a character in a complex learning game and we are in charge of our choices and everyone is there to support that game, then we have the power to love and forgive and change the game.

The more we love and forgive others the faster we learn our lessons and can move on to the next level. We can also control how others treat us by changing our mental picture and energy that we have about them. Ho'oponopono is the way to change how they treat us because it changes the energy between us. I have used this on people who hate me and have wronged me. I haven't spoken a word to them to help them change. I just worked on my idea and picture of them. I would focus on them and the energy I had about what had happened and I would say, I'm sorry, please forgive me, I love you, thank you. I would say this over and over in my mind while thinking of them. I would try to feel the emotion with every word.

Each part of the words of Ho'oponopono utilizes the Godhead.

I'm sorry brings you in humility. You are no longer angry or hurt, you no longer let this experience define who you are. You are sorry for letting this control you or you are sorry for your actions, either way, you are coming to the altar in humility. Your "ego" and "pain-body" are checked at the door only humility accompanies you forward to this sacred rite.

Please forgive me calls upon the atonement of Jesus Christ. It uses the power of his ultimate sacrifice to cleans and erases the energy surrounding the event and memory that is keeping you stuck. Using the ultimate power of forgiveness can transmute any negative energy stuck in your subconscious that is keeping you in a pattern.

I love you calls upon the power of God and His unconditional love. Unconditional love is what you are made of and what your soul desperately wants to remember. It heals all, physically and spiritually. It fills every hole and emptiness in your soul and completes you. It can change all from addiction to self-loathing, from physical ailments to a broken spirit. It brings us home.

Thank You calls upon the Holy Spirit in the form of gratitude. The universe and God give you more of what you focus on and when you are focused on gratitude you will receive more of what you are grateful for. By allowing the energy of gratitude we allow abundance. When we are grateful for what we have we remove the energetic blocks that keep abundance from us.

What other areas can you apply this healing miracle? Have you considered your relationship with money could benefit with <u>Ho'oponopono</u>, what about your possessions, your car, your washing machine? If everything is energy and everything is part of your game, why can you not affect everything with love and forgiveness?

Christ said we could command the mountain to move if we had faith the grain of a mustard seed. We often pray to the Lord to bless us and prosper us and then we sit back and wait. What if you can do something to help the Lord? Pray and ask and then send Ho'oponopono love to what you are praying about. We know that each of those things works. The Lord blesses the servant who is grateful with even more.

Rule #6: Know thyself, thy "whole self" the light and the darkness. Love both sides of the coin.

I think this is the main reason we came to this earthly life. We wanted to know our own souls on a deeper level. We wanted to understand all and know all. We wanted to go deep and experience things we could never experience in our pre-earth life. To do this we needed contrast. We needed to have a shadow side to our light, we needed to make mistakes, and grow from them. The plan is beautiful, know love and forgive thyself.

Rule #7: What we understand the nature of God to be is our limitation. What our minds hold as beliefs and truths, is the framework of our limitations. The details of our limitations are based in memory and experience. This makes up our limiting truth.

Our limiting truth is also what forms our prejudices and feeds our ego we must be right. We go to great lengths to prove how right our belief system is.

Throughout history, man has gone to war over his limited beliefs. Man killed other men because their belief of God was different than others beliefs. They, therefore, must be bad and wrong and deserve to die or at least not to go to as good as heaven as where you are going.

Examine your own limited beliefs. Do you have blinders on and are closed to every way and every path but the one you believe to be true? Do you think you are going to be exalted over others because of your beliefs? Can you set them aside and love all paths that are good and lead to God? Can you accept and open your mind that God's ways are not your ways. God's ways are higher. This doesn't mean you have to abandon your path but open your mind and heart to God and all of heaven's expressions of love. Listen to God and his whisperings in your heart, of your highest path, and accept and love others along their path.

Our unlimited truth is being open to God and all of heaven's expressions of love. Accepting and loving what is, combined with "being" is our "Heaven on Earth or Nirvana" state.

Jesus Christ said, John 14:12 Aramaic Bible in Plain English
"Timeless truth, I tell you: 'whoever believes in me, those works which I have done he will also do, and he will do greater works than these because I am going to the presence of my Father.'

Chapter 43
Unleash your highest self.

I believe you are an angel or what we perceive angels to be. You are royalty a son or daughter of the most high God. Your spirit is perfect love. You are enough and have always been enough. There is nothing you need to try harder to become because you are already that what you seek.

You just need to quit blocking yourself remembering your inner angel. We are a perfect spiritual being having a temporary physical experience, a beautiful physical experience that we couldn't wait to have. We knew it would give us contrast, and a point of reference to fulfill us and help us be grateful.

Space and emptiness define the things it surrounds. If we didn't have empty space everything would be one ball of undefined matter. The space around something defines what that matter is. The contrast of what we are is best described as sin, sorrow, pain or suffering alongside the joy, light, love, compassion, and hope. That duality helps give you shape helps define what you are. It is such a necessary part of the realization of our soul and becoming more.

Much like the story of Adam and Eve partaking of the fruit of the tree of knowledge of good and evil, our partaking of this life, it's disappointments, sorrow, sin, and corruption, our becoming physical and experiencing the knowledge of the opposite of light and love is the most beautiful lesson we could ask to receive.

It defines us. It helps us transcend past the limited knowledge we had, after this life, we become more. I imagine it's like a caterpillar becoming a butterfly. It is a very painful process, but what we were pre-earth; "spirit" was like the caterpillar, this life is the chrysalis and after this life, we become so much more than we were before because of the transformation.

You can embrace the process by allowing the love and knowledge of what you are here to speed up the process of transformation or you can block the process by refusing to forgive yourself and remember into being what you are. If you continue to block and refuse to forgive you stay in the "in-between state" or chrysalis state.

This state is full of self-doubt, anger, depression, pain, and suffering. What if because you refuse to transform when you die you get to do it again. What if the universe and God only know how to say yes. Yes to allow us to progress and learn over and over until you get it right? Because there is no time for God we could theoretically exist in multiple lives at one moment from God's perspective.

I know that hurts my head to think about, but whether it's true or not true has no bearing on this life you are living now. The transformation is real. The fact that you are part of God is true, whether it's we are his children, or parts of a whole experiencing itself, or any of the other theories that point to the truth that we are light, love, and part of a loving higher power I call Father or God.

I testify what I experienced in meeting God after I was electrocuted was love. I testify that there is an afterlife, and that God exists and that all I experienced was love and fulfillment in God's presence, not judgment. How I choose to interpret what happened to me is about my experience. How you choose to interpret what I say is about yours. I don't believe that you are wrong or I am wrong. There is only our experience that helps with our transformation.

If what I say causes you to ponder on the nature of God, develop a relationship, or start the process of forgiving yourself and realizing that you are divine, then I have succeeded in my purpose. Maybe only part of my message rings true for you or maybe it all does, I challenge you to take the seed and use it to propel you toward your own truth and purpose. My purpose is to undergo my own transition remembering into love and serve those that I can uplift and help in their transformation.

Mahalo
Ryan Rampton
11-15-18

Made in United States
Orlando, FL
23 March 2023

31343928R00139